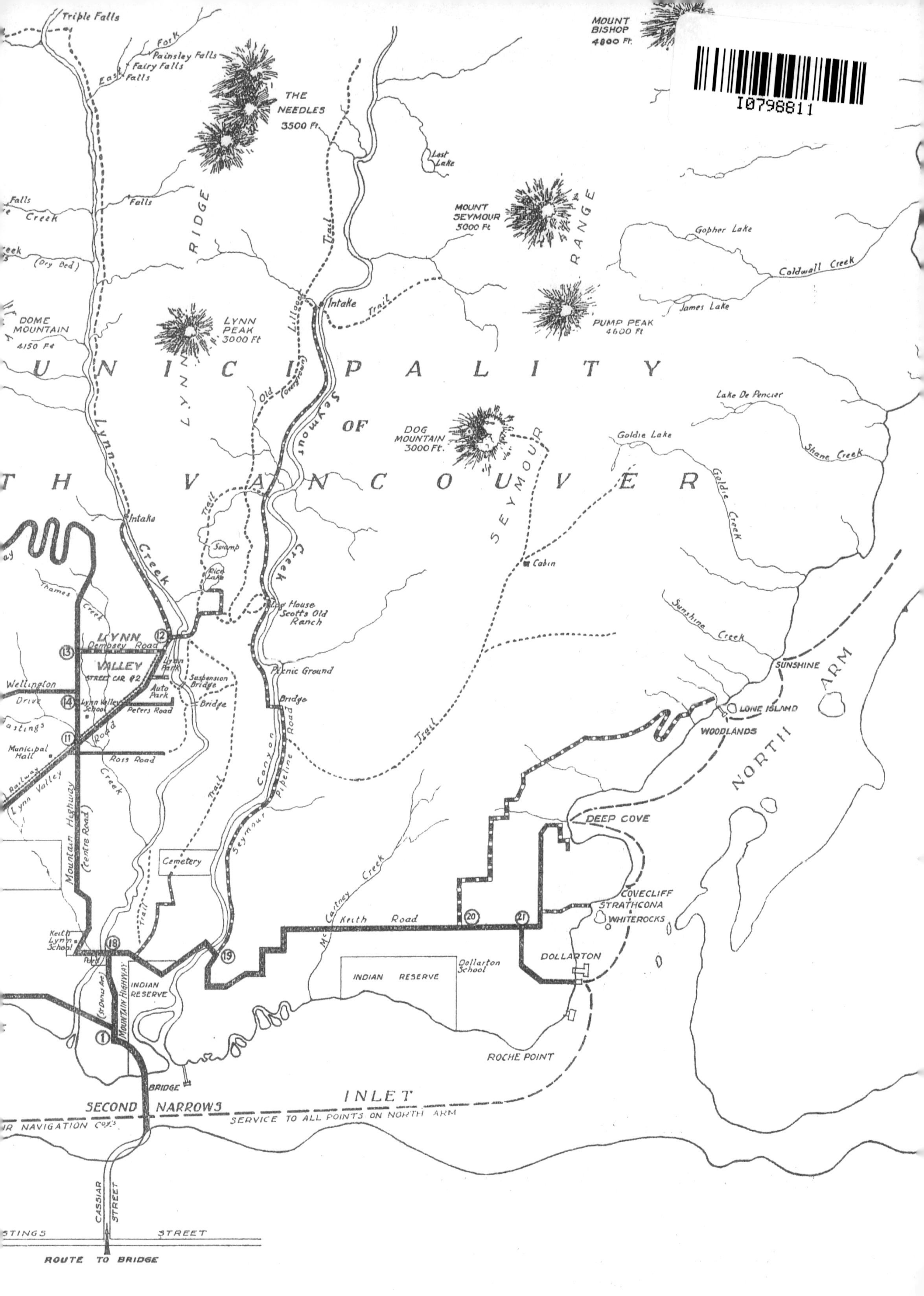

Triple Falls
Fork
Painsley Falls
Fairy Falls
East Falls
THE NEEDLES 3500 Ft
MOUNT BISHOP 4800 Ft.
Lost Lake
MOUNT SEYMOUR 5000 Ft
RANGE
Gopher Lake
Coldwall Creek
James Lake
PUMP PEAK 4600 Ft
Falls
Creek
(Dry Bed)
RIDGE
LYNN
DOME MOUNTAIN 4150 Ft
LYNN PEAK 3000 Ft
Intake
Trail
Lillooet
Old (overgrown)
UNICIPALITY
OF
TH VANCOUVER
Seymour
DOG MOUNTAIN 3000 Ft.
SEYMOUR
Lake De Pencier
Goldie Lake
Shane Creek
Goldie Creek
Lynn
Intake
Creek
Swamp
Rice Lake
Log House Scotts Old Ranch
Creek
Cabin
Sunshine Creek
Thames Creek
LYNN
Dempsey Road
VALLEY
STREET CAR #2
Lynn Park
Suspension Bridge
Auto Park
Bridge
Peters Road
Lynn Valley School
Wellington Drive
Hastings
Municipal Hall
Road
Ross Road
Creek
Railway
Lynn Valley
Picnic Ground
Bridge
Canyon
Pipeline Road
Trail
SUNSHINE
LONE ISLAND
WOODLANDS
NORTH ARM
Trail
Seymour
Cemetery
Mountain Highway (Centre Road)
McCartney Creek
DEEP COVE
COVECLIFF
STRATHCONA
WHITEROCKS
Keith Road
Keith Lynn School
Park
INDIAN RESERVE
(St Denis Ave)
MOUNTAIN HIGHWAY
INDIAN RESERVE
Dollarton School
DOLLARTON
ROCHE POINT
BRIDGE
SECOND NARROWS
INLET
R NAVIGATION Co's
SERVICE TO ALL POINTS ON NORTH ARM
CASSIAR STREET
STINGS STREET
ROUTE TO BRIDGE

WHERE MOUNTAINS MEET THE SEA

WHERE MOUNTAINS MEET THE SEA

AN ILLUSTRATED HISTORY OF THE DISTRICT OF NORTH VANCOUVER

DANIEL FRANCIS

HARBOUR PUBLISHING

Above: ***North Vancouver #3*** **joined the fleet in 1911.** NVMA 15932

Previous pages: The ferry dock at the foot of Lonsdale Avenue ca. 1906 in a photograph taken from the deck of a departing ferry. The tiny community is on the verge of incorporating as the City of North Vancouver. NVMA 190

CONTENTS

Above: A panoramic view of the North Vancouver waterfront in 1917 shows the ferry wharf and Wallace Shipyards, where so many wartime vessels were built, to the right. NVMA 1479

Foreword

Mayor Richard Walton

North Vancouver District was created on August 10, 1891, with the incorporation of lands stretching from Horseshoe Bay to Deep Cove. Our human history here begins much earlier, however, with the Squamish and Tsleil-Waututh peoples, whose traditional territories extend far beyond our modern boundaries and whose ancestors made their homes here thousands of years before European explorers arrived in 1791.

At that time a series of tidal flats stretched from the mouth of the Capilano River, at the First Narrows where the Lions Gate Bridge now stands, eastward to the Mosquito Creek estuary at the foot of today's Bewicke Avenue. The clear waters from the North Shore Mountains flowed into Burrard Inlet through nutrient-rich marshlands. East of Mosquito Creek, steeper terrain and deeper waters extended across what was then the sawmill community of Moodyville (now the City of North Vancouver waterfront), to the next set of tidal estuaries where Lynn Creek and the Seymour River flow side by side into the inlet at the Second Narrows. Within this area, the Maplewood Flats Conservation Area is now the last remnant of the once-extensive tidal flats.

With the arrival of industry on the North Shore in the 1860s, and the arrival of the Canadian Pacific Railway a generation later, life and the landscape changed at an ever-accelerating pace. Within fifty years railway berms and dredged infill created man-made shorelines that damaged the tidal estuaries. The skies darkened with pollution from sawmills and unfettered wood-waste burners, and the North Shore mountainsides were stripped of their original old-growth trees. And yet, over the years, a growing realization spread that this place is a living paradise. Although we cannot turn back history, the past few decades have seen the emergence of a culture of environmental awareness, stewardship and balance that is very encouraging.

Today North Vancouver's vibrant waterfront and port facilities ship and receive more goods than any other city in Canada. And while the river mouths have been channelled and the normal flood cycles of mountain creeks have been altered to facilitate bridge abutments, dry basements in our homes and the protection of vital municipal infrastructure, recent positive human intervention has seen the salmon return to our streams and a community celebration of our natural heritage. The early perception of the North Shore forests only having value for loggers and entrepreneurs has shifted over time. In 1889, the first Capilano Suspension Bridge, which would become one of Canada's major tourist attractions, got its start hosting visitors and residents already waking up to the natural beauty on their doorstep.

Left: The Lynn Canyon suspension bridge has been part of Lynn Canyon Park ever since the District opened it as a public attraction in 1912. NVMA 5216

A trio of hikers enjoys an outing on Grouse Mountain, 1901. The photograph was taken by Claire Downing, a businessman and amateur photographer. Many of his images chronicle the early days of outdoor recreation on the North Shore. VPL 4836

Recently we have come to realize that the landscape of the North Shore largely defines how we see ourselves: close to nature with a vast wilderness at our doorstep, with the benefits of being part of a large adjacent urban area. And over the years we have shifted from being a bedroom community of commuters facing south, to a community of wilderness lovers on the edge of a metropolis looking north.

The North Shore consistently ranks among the healthiest regions in Canada to live, work and play, and we are among the best educated and safest communities as well. International companies locate here because this is where key employees wish to raise their families. The resurgence of shipbuilding ensures the continuance of well-paid waterfront jobs, located in a community that appreciates and supports industry.

And we will continue to be vigilant as a community, as newer local and global challenges related to housing affordability, transportation congestion and climate change face us. We can celebrate the good things we have achieved while we plan carefully for the

Streetcar No. 152 on the Lynn Valley line. By the time this photograph was taken in 1913, riders could take the street railway from the ferry wharf all the way almost to the top of Lynn Valley Road. NVMA 6554

future. Although our initial economic prosperity brought along with it environmental compromises, we are well on our way to achieving the careful balance that healthy communities achieve.

Our community is unique: we have subalpine highlands located only minutes away from world-class port facilities and industry; we have wildlife in our backyards, yet are only a short bus ride from downtown Vancouver. The North Shore is the interface between the urban core and the wilderness, and that is the magic that defines our community and who we are.

Where Mountains Meet the Sea tells our story. What better way is there to celebrate our 125th anniversary than sitting down with a good book to learn about ourselves? And learning about our past provides a great foundation for getting involved in the future. Our natural shorelines may be forever changed, but the community's love, respect and appreciation for our natural heritage and way of life continue to grow.

MABEL BROWN
378.

Introduction

People have inhabited the North Shore of Burrard Inlet for thousands of years, harvesting the rich resources of land and sea. With the arrival of the early explorers, followed by Euro-Canadian settlers, the slopes of the North Shore Mountains with their magnificent stands of tall timber attracted the attention of loggers, sawmillers and shipbuilders. The inlet's long shoreline and deepwater harbour allowed these industries to thrive and form the basis of the community of North Vancouver, which now partners with Vancouver as Canada's Pacific gateway.

The ferry *St. George*, launched in 1904, was named for the real estate developer Alfred St. George Hamersley. It was renamed *North Vancouver #2* when the service was taken over by the city. NVMA 10017

In 2016 the District of North Vancouver celebrates its 125th anniversary. To mark this important milestone, the North Vancouver Museum & Archives decided it was important to produce an up-to-date history of the community. *Where Mountains Meet the Sea* tells the story of the North Shore from its original First Nations inhabitants to its newest newcomers, from its industrial waterfront to the snow-covered slopes of its mountain resorts. When it was incorporated in 1891, the District of North Vancouver included the north side of Burrard Inlet from Horseshoe Bay on the west to Indian Arm on the east. In 1907 the City of North Vancouver was created as a separate municipality encompassing the central core of the District. Then, in 1912, the community of West Vancouver was created, setting apart the area west of the Capilano River. For many years North Vancouver slumbered. It had many assets. Its mountain slopes attracted hikers and skiers; loggers exploited its rich forests; its shipyards gave jobs to thousands of workers, especially during wartime. But residential settlement was patchy and slow to develop and the community remained a suburb of Vancouver for the first half of its history. Following World War II, however, a new era dawned. With two new bridges providing access to Vancouver across the inlet, North Vancouver emerged as a residential community in its own right. Small, isolated neighbourhoods were joined by new suburban developments until by the 1970s the disparate parts of North Vancouver were coming together to form a growing, prosperous mountainside community.

Left: The *Mabel Brown*, first of a series of wooden schooners built at Wallace Shipyards on the North Vancouver waterfront during World War I. NVMA 4973

Squamish Chief Simon Baker (centre) performing traditional dances with Chief Mathias Joe Capilano (l.) and Dominic Charlie (r.) in 1958. NVMA 10525

The organization of the contents of *Where Mountains Meet the Sea* requires a word of explanation. Instead of the conventional chronology, the material is divided into three chapters, each dealing with one of three important themes: the waterfront, the growth of the community and the natural environment. Within each chapter the content moves more or less chronologically but overall the content moves geographically from the waterfront up the sides of the mountain slopes. Chapter 1, "On the Waterfront," focuses on the original First Nations inhabitants, transportation networks around Burrard Inlet and the development of waterfront industries. Chapter 2, "Building Communities," describes the political, social and cultural evolution of the North Shore and the development of its various neighbourhoods. Finally, Chapter 3, "On Nature's Edge," describes North Vancouver's rich legacy of wilderness and parks.

An aerial view of North Vancouver illustrates how the community has spread away from its industrial waterfront up the mountain slopes to the wilderness alpine areas beyond. Bob Smit photo

At the beginning of the twenty-first century, North Vancouver entered a period of unprecedented growth, with all the opportunities and challenges that development presents. The 125th anniversary seems an appropriate vantage point from which to look back on the entire history of the community to understand how it arrived at where it is today.

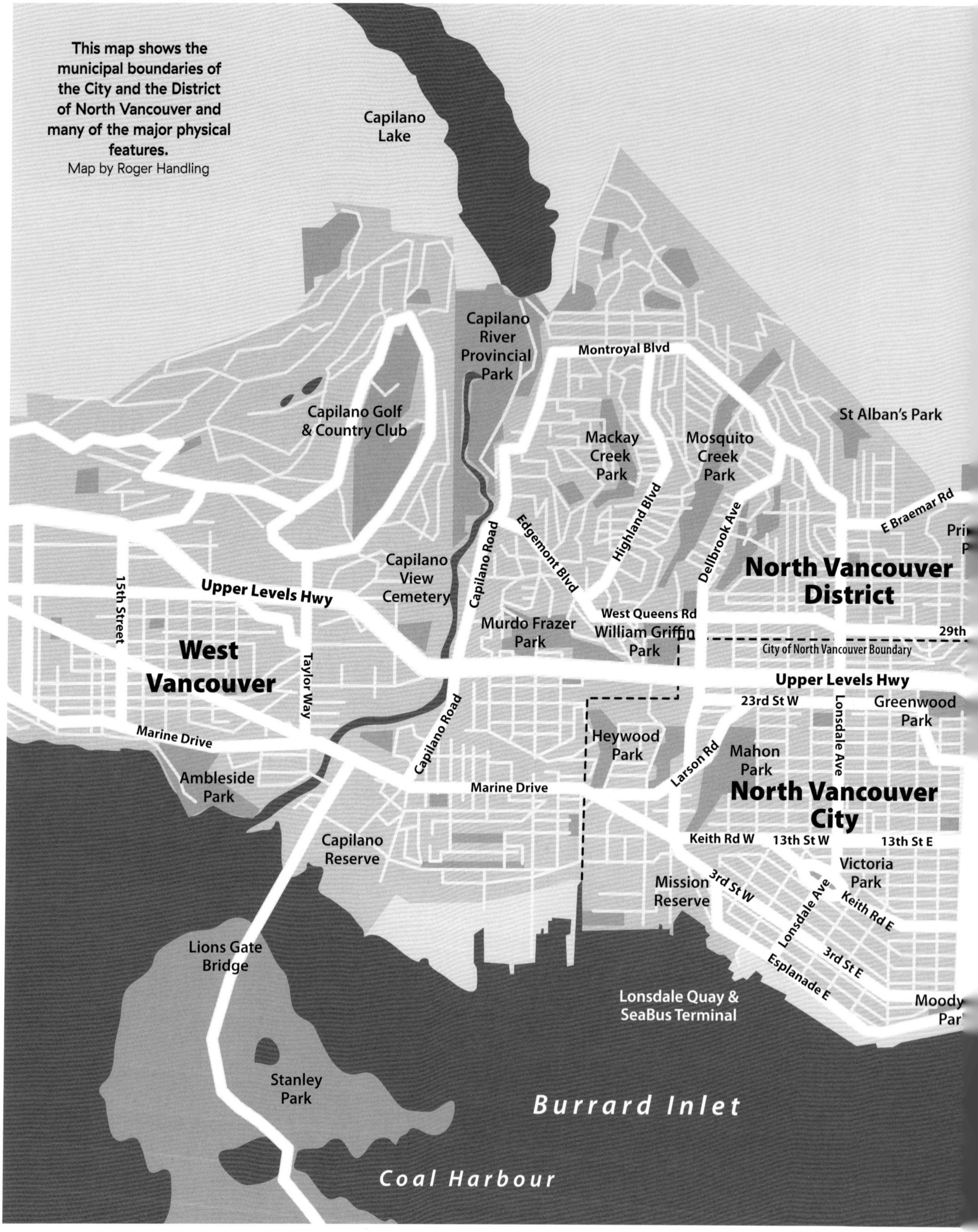

This map shows the municipal boundaries of the City and the District of North Vancouver and many of the major physical features.
Map by Roger Handling

nn Headwaters
Regional Park
0 km
1 km
Approx. scale
Lynn Valley Rd
Mount Seymour
Provincial Park
Dempsey Rd
Mountain Hwy
Lillooet Rd
Valley Rd
Lynn Canyon
Park
Kirkstone
Park
Hastings
Creek Park
Canyon
Creek Park
Mt Seymour Rd
Mountain Hwy
Deep Cove
North Vancouver
Cemetery
Inter-River
Park
McCartney
Creek Park
Northlands
Golf Course
Myrtle
Park
Capilano
University
Mt Seymour Pkwy
Rd E
Seymour Golf
& Country Club
Dollarton Hwy N
Tsleil – Waututh
Nation
Seymour
Creek
Reserve
Mt Seymour Pkwy
Dollarton Hwy
Cotton Dr
Main St
Maplewood
Farm
Dollarton Hwy
Cates Park
Second Narrows

ON THE WATERFRONT

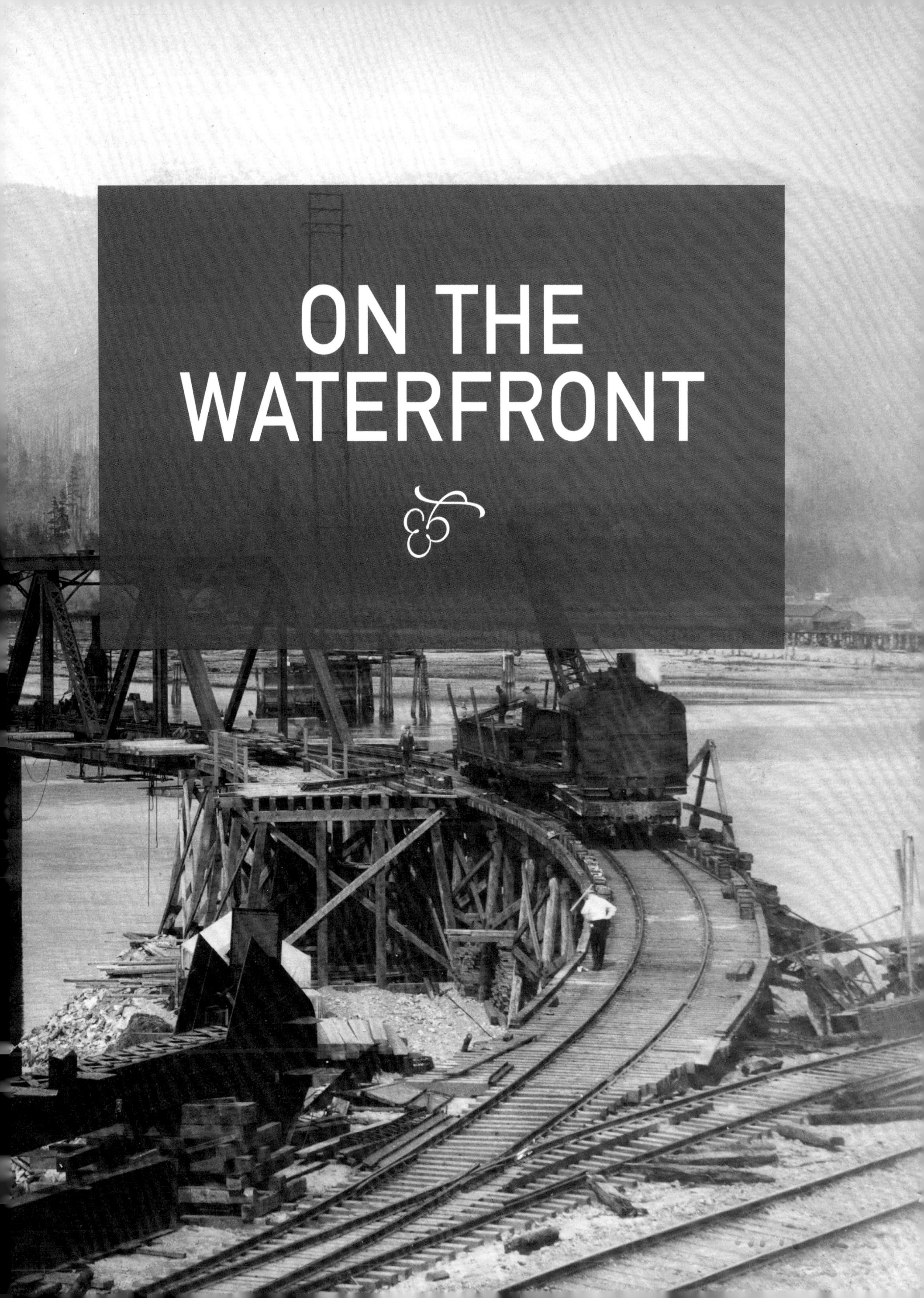

In 1792, the year that European explorers first entered Burrard Inlet and saw the shores of what would become North Vancouver, the northwest coast of North America was only beginning to take shape on the maps of the world. Spanish and British mariners had been probing the coves and inlets of the coast for several years, seeking the fabled Northwest Passage that would connect the Atlantic and Pacific oceans across the top of America. In the process they launched a thriving trade in sea otter pelts and began to understand the convoluted geography of the place.

It was one of these probes that brought José María Narváez, a twenty-three-year-old Spanish navigator, within sight of the North Shore Mountains on a July afternoon in 1791. Narváez commanded forty-one officers and crew aboard the 11-metre schooner *Santa Saturnina*. These mariners became the first Europeans to set eyes on the Salish Sea, what they called the "Gran Canal." Crossing from the Gulf Islands to the eastern side of the Strait, Narváez and his men cruised past the mouth of the Fraser River and anchored off Point Grey, where they made contact with several canoes from the Musqueam villages

Above: A Squamish carving depicting Thunderbird and Otter. NVMA 1986.019.0079

Preceding pages: The original Second Narrows Bridge nears completion in the spring of 1925. NVMA 9736

> "As your great explorer Vancouver progressed through the First Narrows, our people threw in greeting before him clouds of snow white feathers which rose, wafted in the air aimlessly about, then fell like flurries of snow to the water's surface, and rested there like white rose petals scattered before a bride. It must have been a pretty welcome."
> —Andrew Paull, Squamish leader, 1932[1]

at the river's mouth. Then, on July 9, the Spanish vessel neared the shore of what is now West Vancouver, pausing just outside the First Narrows. Narváez decided against entering the narrow passage, but he may have sent his longboat to visit the Squamish village of Homulcheson (Xwemelch'stn) at the mouth of the Capilano River. Regardless, he identified the inner inlet as a possible avenue to the trans-continental passage—what the Spanish called the "Strait of Anian"—before he sailed away north to continue his investigations of the Gran Canal. Assuming that the weather was clear, Narváez and his men were the first Europeans to get a glimpse of the North Shore.

The following summer another European expedition appeared in Burrard Inlet in search of the Northwest Passage. This time it was the British who were taking their turn. Captain George Vancouver and his men had left their mother ships, *Discovery* and *Chatham*, anchored in Birch Bay and were travelling in two ship's boats. Unlike

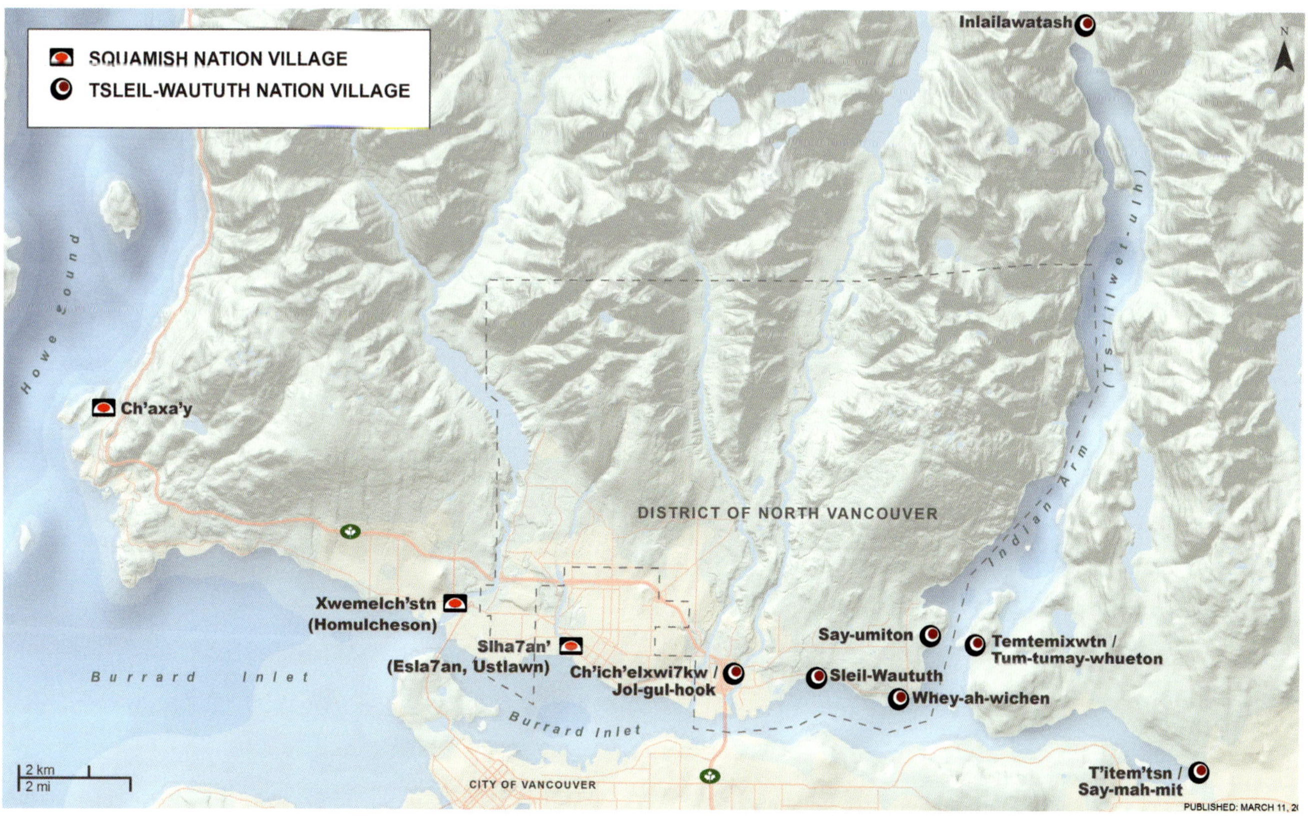

This map shows First Nations names for several North Shore sites, including (from west to east) Horseshoe Bay, Capilano Reserve, Mission Reserve, Seymour River, Burrard Reserve, Cates Park, Cove Cliff and Belcarra.

Narváez, Vancouver did not hesitate to enter the narrows. On June 12, 1792, as they rowed past what is now Stanley Park, a party of about fifty Squamish people came out to meet them. These people, recorded Vancouver, "conducted themselves with the greatest decorum and civility, presenting us with several fish . . ."[2] As the British carried out their investigation of the inlet as far as Indian Arm, a few of the local people followed in canoes. After camping for the night, Vancouver and his men returned through the First Narrows and along the shore before rounding Point Atkinson into Howe Sound to continue their survey.

Nine days later another party of Spanish mariners appeared in Burrard Inlet, following up on the explorations of their countryman Narváez from the summer before. The boats came from two ships anchored near Point Grey, the *Sutil*, commanded by Dionisio Alcalá Galiano, and the *Mexicana*, under Cayetano Valdés. They travelled to the head of Indian Arm, where they encountered a camp of Tsleil-Waututh people with whom they had a short meeting. "The mild temperature, the beauty and lushness of the various greens, the multitude of clusters of wild roses, and several meadows with small fruits, blackberries and gooseberries, made it a delightful visit," recorded Galiano.[3] Then the Spanish retraced their steps and left the inlet.

This early photograph shows a group of Squamish dwellings on the shores of Burrard Inlet at about the time that the first non-Aboriginal settlers began to take an interest in the inlet's forest resources.
CVA AM54-S4-: St Pk N4

These episodes are the first written accounts we have of North Vancouver and its indigenous inhabitants. When they arrived on the Northwest Coast, the Europeans thought they were exploring an isolated wilderness at the very edge of the known world. To the First Nations, however, the coast was their home. It was the centre, not the margin. The Coast Salish people, the Squamish and the Tsleil-Waututh, used Burrard Inlet to fish, gather shellfish, and hunt waterfowl and seal. On the slopes of the mountainsides they tracked deer, bear and smaller animals, gathered fruits and edible plants and obtained the wood they used to manufacture their homes, canoes, utensils and monumental art. The south coast of what is now British Columbia was the location of their history and the source of their livelihood and their spirituality. It also had been much more densely populated than it was when the outsiders first appeared. A smallpox epidemic with its origins in Mexico swept through the southern coast in the early 1780s, killing as much as 80 percent of the population in some areas. It was followed by successive waves of disease, each taking a terrible toll. By some accounts the Tsleil-Waututh, for example, numbered about ten thousand people pre-contact. That figure plummeted to one hundred individuals by the 1830s. The Squamish suffered a comparable decline. George Vancouver remarked on the number of deserted villages he and his officers observed. The world that the Spanish and British navigators entered was not the same world they would have seen just a few years earlier.

THE FIRST NATIONS OF NORTH VANCOUVER

The Squamish and the Tsleil-Waututh are related but distinct First Nations belonging to the Coast Salish family of cultural groups. The Tsleil-Waututh traditionally spoke a dialect of the Halkomelem language, Halq'eméylem, used by nations of the Fraser Valley and south-eastern Vancouver Island, while the Squamish spoke a distinct variant of Coast Salish. The two groups are also related culturally to, but distinct from, the Musqueam in Vancouver. All three groups share overlapping traditional territories and land claims. Today the registered Squamish population numbers about 4,100 people, the Tsleil-Waututh about 580 and the Musqueam about 1,375.

The Rise of Moodyville

Following these brief encounters between European explorers and First Nations residents, outsiders did not return to Burrard Inlet for several decades. When they did, it was to exploit the rich stands of timber that blanketed its shores. The discovery of gold in the Fraser River brought an influx of miners to the mainland in 1858 and led to the creation of the colony of British Columbia along with a new capital city, Queensborough (later New Westminster). But all this activity bypassed Burrard Inlet, which remained away from the beaten path. Things finally changed in 1863 when Pioneer Mills began producing lumber at its plant on the North

The Moodyville waterfront during the 1880s. Moodyville was the first settler community on the shores of Burrard Inlet. NVMA 6604

Shore, about 6.5 kilometres to the east of the First Narrows. The site lay at the foot of a steep escarpment near the mouth of what is now Lynn Creek, surrounded by thousands of hectares of dense forest of the finest cedar and fir. The mill, started by a pair of builders from New Westminster, was the first industrial plant in the inlet and the beginning of settlement by outsiders.

Despite its advantages, Pioneer Mills got off to a rough start. Unable to compete in the limited local market with mills in New Westminster, the original owners sold out within six months. The business reopened in the spring of 1864 under new ownership as Burrard Inlet Mills and managed to

Above: The hotel at Moodyville in 1886, owned originally by Captain William Power. NVMA 5056

Right: The community of Moodyville spread up the slope behind the waterfront mill where ships from around the world loaded timber. VPL 3392

A few of the town's big shots gather on the wharf at Moodyville, ca. 1889. NVMA 13377

dispatch its first foreign shipments of lumber to Chile and Australia before once again falling into bankruptcy. It was at this point that a saviour appeared in the form of an aspiring lumberman named Sewell "Sue" Prescott Moody. Moody, who was American by birth and a devout Methodist by inclination, snapped up the mill at auction, along with the rights to 195 hectares of timber. By February 1865 he and his partners had it back in production. Within two years the mill had acquired the rights to more than 4,000 hectares of timber and was exporting lumber to countries around the Pacific Rim and to Great Britain. Logs arrived from camps located at several places on the North Shore, including Deep Cove, Lynn Creek, the Capilano River and Ambleside. Moody added a steam plant to replace the water-driven saws, and wharves to handle the deep-sea vessels. Once British Columbia joined the rest of Canada in Confederation in 1871, his mill was the single largest source of export revenue in the province. The operation had different names but was known locally as "Moody's Mill" and the community which grew up around it, "Moodyville." (The name is attributed to a suggestion by schoolteacher Margaret Thain.)

In the early years, the only other communities on the North Shore were First Nations. At the time of contact the Squamish probably did not occupy permanent villages in Burrard Inlet, perhaps with the exception of Homulcheson at the mouth of the Capilano River. Their over-wintering sites were located in Howe Sound and the valley of the Squamish River. But sometime around 1830 a long-standing conflict with more northerly groups ended and, no longer threatened by raids from the north, the Squamish

Top: St. Paul's Roman Catholic Church on the Mission Reserve, the oldest surviving mission church in Greater Vancouver, shown here in the 1890s, was designated a National Historic Site in 1980. NVMA WN.040. Courtesy of William Nahanee

Bottom: Group of Squamish men from the Mission Reserve pose inside a canoe they have been building, ca. 1912. NVMA 4845

felt more secure about living permanently in Burrard Inlet. This shift in settlement patterns was reinforced with the opening of sawmills at Moodyville and Granville, the future site of Vancouver, during the 1860s. Many of the First Nations people found work at the mills as loggers and stevedores, loading the timber onto the ships that carried it across the globe. The proximity of these employment opportunities was an added incentive for the people to settle year-round. Ustlawn (Eslhá7an), located

A view of the Squamish village of Ustlawn in 1886. It was also called the "Mission Reserve" because Catholic missionaries had built the church, St. Paul's, visible in the centre of the photograph. CVA AM54–S4 SGN1460

This group of longshoremen on the Moodyville waterfront in 1889, some of them First Nations men, illustrates the multi-ethnic makeup of the mill workforce. William Nahanee, whose mother was from Homulcheson, poses with a bag of laundry. City of Vancouver Archives MiP2

at the mouth of Mosquito Creek, had long been used as a seasonal camp by the Squamish, but during the 1860s, more families began to live there permanently. Aside from job opportunities, another reason for this shift was the presence of a Catholic church which the Oblate priest Leon Fouquet built at Ustlawn in 1866. In November 1869, at the insistence of Chief Snatt, the community's leader, 35 acres (14 ha) of this land was formally gazetted as Indian Reserve #1. At the same time, the Tsleil-Waututh village site farther east near Roche Point was set aside as Indian Reserve #3. Archaeological evidence suggests that the Tsleil-Waututh ("People of the Inlet") have occupied village sites around Roche Point and Belcarra for 3,500 years. Prior to the mid-1800s they were probably the only permanent residents of Burrard Inlet (as distinct from seasonal visitors). Their main winter settlement was Temtemixwtn, located at what is now Belcarra, but they maintained other villages and camps around the inlet, including the site designated as Indian Reserve #3. Several years later the federal and provincial governments, which had yet to resolve the issue of Aboriginal land rights in the province, appointed the Joint Indian Reserve Commission to do just that. The three-person commission, led by Gilbert Malcolm Sproat, visited the various First Nations and designated reserves for them. On November 11, 1876, the commissioners camped at Homulcheson at the mouth of the Capilano River and began their meetings with the First Nations of Burrard Inlet. By the time they moved on a few days later, they had confirmed Ustlawn as Indian Reserve #1, along with reserve sites at Homulcheson, Seymour Creek (chi'ch'elxwikw') and the Tsleil-Waututh village farther east. According to a census undertaken by the commission, there were 123 people living at the Mission Reserve at Ustlawn, 41 people at Homulcheson, 22 at Seymour and 39 at the Burrard, or Tsleil-Waututh, Reserve. One of the reserve commissioners noted, "Many of the Indians are excellent workmen. They are employed

THE BOWS AND ARROWS

Longshoring became associated with the First Nations of the North Shore. Squamish and Tsleil-Waututh men commonly found jobs on the waterfront loading ships. Many of these men—such as Joe Capilano (Sahp-luk) and Dan George (Geswanouth Slahoot)—were prominent leaders in their communities. In 1906 a core group of First Nations lumber loaders formed Local 526 of the Industrial Workers of the World. The local, the Lumber Handlers Union, came to be called the "Bows and Arrows" and persisted in one form or another for several decades, promoting better wages and working conditions on the waterfront.

Top: Ships loading lumber at the Moodyville mill during the 1870s when the small community was the capital of Burrard Inlet. NVMA 3779

Bottom: The Star Gang, a group of mainly First Nations longshoremen who worked the Moodyville waterfront. NVMA 4846 in loading vessels and in general work about the sawmills. Several of them work inside the mills. They receive from 75 cents a day with food and lodging to $1¼ or $1½ a day without food and lodging. A ready market exists at the mills for whatever fish and game the Indians bring in."[4] In other words, aside from their own traditional activities, the First Nations were active participants in the emerging economy of Burrard Inlet.

> **"They had a jailhouse in Moodyville too. Sue [Moody] had it built. If you got too rough, they put you in there behind bars."**
> **—Axel Nyman, retired longshoreman[5]**

Meanwhile the population at Moodyville hovered around two hundred. Mostly employees of the mill, it was a diverse group of Africans, Chinese, Polynesians, Chileans and Europeans from various countries. Small as it was, the community thrived under the leadership of "Sue" Moody and, after his death, the new mill manager Hugh Nelson. For nearly twenty years it was the leading community on the inlet and home to many "firsts." In June 1865, for instance, Reverend Ebenezer Robson, a Methodist preacher from New Westminster, arrived to conduct the first organized religious service for white residents of the inlet. A Mechanics' Institute opened at the beginning of 1869, offering the first library and reading room, even a small museum, while the first school opened in 1870. (After one inspection the school superintendent reported that sometimes school had to be dismissed because smoke from the sawmill leaked in under the door.) Electricity arrived in 1882, providing the first electric lights north of San Francisco. The community had its own newspaper, the *Moodyville Tickler*, a two-storey hotel and a general store that served customers from all around the inlet. There was no hospital but there was a nurse, Mrs. Emily Patterson, who served as a midwife and travelled back and forth across the inlet treating the sick and the wounded, white and Aboriginal alike, despite her lack of formal training. Hugh Nelson built an elegant home, Invermere, on the bluff overlooking the mill (known as "Nob Hill") where the cream of local society gathered for tennis parties, croquet and tea. When Nelson retired in 1882, Benjamin Springer became the mill manager and moved into Invermere with his wife Frances, who quickly established herself as the leader of the inlet's social elite, hosting elaborate house parties which, on at least one occasion, featured a full orchestra.

> **"There is a library with papers and reading room which is a great boon and places Moodyville far ahead of the neighbouring mills and villages which nearly all boast of a rum mill or two while nothing of the kind is allowed on Moody's land."**
> **—James McCulley, millhand, 1875[6]**

Moodyville's future as the "capital" of Burrard Inlet seemed assured. Square-rigged sailing ships from around the world visited its docks and the sounds of industry echoed across the water. Hugh Nelson even hoped that the little mill town would become the Pacific terminus of the transcontinental Canadian Pacific Railway (CPR). But that was not to be. In 1885 William Van Horne, the CPR's general manager, chose the townsite of Granville on the south shore to be the railway's terminus. Incorporated as the City of Vancouver in 1886, the site soon outpaced its rival across the inlet. The Moodyville company struggled to cope with the economic downturn that hit the province during the 1890s. As the most accessible stands of timber disappeared, the business declined. The mill went into receivership in 1897 and closed for good in 1901.

People continued to live in Moodyville, but the commercial centre of the North Shore shifted gradually westward to the foot of Lonsdale Avenue, then a mere trail through the woods. Residents slowly drifted away from the sawmill site and the post office and the school closed. Finally, during World War I, the surviving mill buildings were destroyed by fire and the site was abandoned. Part of the steep hillside was later removed to allow construction of what became today's Low Level Road and, at the beginning of 1925, the City of North Vancouver absorbed Moodyville. Railway tracks, grain elevators and deep-sea shipping terminals now cover the flats where North Vancouver's original community once stood.

MASTER OF MOODYVILLE

Sewell Moody, who was born in the state of Maine around 1835, arrived in British Columbia not long after its creation and immersed himself in the business life of New Westminster. In 1862, having made a profit from importing a herd of beef cattle, he formed a small syndicate and built a steam sawmill on the Fraser River. When this first foray into the lumber business failed, he shifted his focus to Burrard Inlet, where he purchased the bankrupt mill on the North Shore that would become the centre of Moodyville.

"Sue" Moody was a staunch Methodist and teetotaller who insisted that, in "his" town, nobody take a drink. It was also his influence that led to the first school, the first church and the first library all being established in Moodyville. Two days before Christmas in 1873, a fire destroyed half the sawmill. Undeterred, Moody had it rebuilt bigger and better and it was producing lumber again within three months.

Moody met a tragic death. In November 1875 he left Victoria for San Francisco aboard the steamship *Pacific*. Off Cape Flattery, his vessel collided with another ship in the night and sank. Out of 277 people on board, just two survived. The only trace of Moody himself was a piece of board found on the beach near Victoria six weeks later. Scrawled across it in pencil was his last plaintive message: "S. P. Moody—all lost."

Farmers and Gentlemen

Even while the sawmill was healthy and Moodyville was humming with enterprise during the 1870s and 1880s, settlement began to spread along the North Shore waterfront in both directions. To the east, between Lynn Creek and the Seymour River, a Royal Engineer named John Linn settled his family in 1871. The Engineers were a British contingent sent out to British Columbia in 1858 to initiate public works and provide a military presence in the new colony. When they were recalled five years later, many of the men accepted military grants from the government and remained in BC to start new lives for themselves and their families. John Linn was one of these, and the creek beside which he built a home eventually took his name, or a variation of it.

Irishman Hugh Burr, formerly a schoolteacher in New Westminster, settled the land on the east side of the Seymour and eventually owned the stretch of waterfront as far as the Tsleil-Waututh reserve. Burr planted an orchard and operated a dairy farm, the first one on the inlet, from which he supplied Moodyville with milk and fresh produce. His property

Above: Mr. and Mrs. John Linn, pioneer settlers on the North Shore. John Linn was a member of the Royal Engineers before he took up land on Lynn Creek. CVA 371-1257

Right: Navvy Jack Thomas, a West Vancouver pioneer, married a Squamish woman, Row-i-a. Two of their daughers were Emma (l.) and Christine (r.), posing here with an unidentified woman, possibly an aunt. NVMA 5081

West Vancouver pioneer settler John Lawson poses atop a tree stump in 1907, the year he and his family moved to Ambleside. West Vancouver Archives: 202.WVA.LAW is now the heart of the Maplewood Flats. In the other direction, to the west of Moodyville, around the foot of what is now Lonsdale Avenue on what was known as District Lot 271, a former sailor named William Bridge owned a small farm with his First Nations wife. Bridge also supplied milk to the mill town. West of Bridge's property was Ustlawn, the Mission Reserve, beyond which three other waterfront lots were all taken up during the 1870s.

At this point, and until 1912, the community of West Vancouver was known informally as "West Capilano" and the area as far as Horseshoe Bay was part of the District of North Vancouver, which was incorporated as a community in 1891. In West Vancouver, too, the lots along the foreshore were occupied during the last two decades of the century, both by homesteaders and by a variety of small industrial enterprises. At Ambleside the Moodyville mill operated camps from 1870 to 1890, drawing timber from a pair of leases on the west side of the Capilano River, and several independent loggers cut timber at other camps farther west. There were two fish canneries—one in Sandy Cove and another in Eagle Harbour—along with "Navvy Jack" Thomas's gravel operation near the mouth of the Capilano.

Above: Frances Caulfeild dreamed of a planned community for gentlefolk on the rocky slopes above Skunk Cove in West Vancouver. 3362.WVA.PHO

For the most part, though, West Vancouver developed as a residential community, with both permanent residences and summer cottages. Among the pioneer settlers were John Lawson, a retired railwayman who purchased Thomas's property at Ambleside in 1907 and christened it "Hollyburn"; Francis Caulfeild, an English gentleman who purchased close to 400 hectares of land overlooking Skunk Cove and used it to develop an elegantly planned community for wealthy Vancouverites; and Peter Larson, a North Vancouver hotelier who for many years cultivated an estate at what is now Gleneagles Golf Course. All of these pioneers contributed to West Vancouver's reputation as a suburban retreat for the comfortably off, a reputation it maintained after it separated from the District of North Vancouver in 1912 to form its own municipality. Residents of West Vancouver observed the hustle and bustle of the North Vancouver waterfront inside the First Narrows and decided they wanted to protect their community from industrial development. This decision is reflected in the contrasting character of the two communities down to the present day. With no manufacturing and little or no industry of any kind, West Vancouver's economy relies on retail and residential developments, while North Vancouver is home to many large industrial facilities associated with the bustling Vancouver harbour, the fourth largest in North America.

DELEGATION TO THE KING

Su-a-pu-luck, also known as "Sahp-luk" or "Joe Capilano," was a leading member of the Squamish Nation at the turn of the twentieth century. Like many Squamish men, he worked as a longshoreman at Moodyville and the Hastings Mill, where he was known for his strength and became a foreman. He was a vocal advocate of First Nations' title to their lands. In the summer of 1906 he and two other chiefs travelled by train to Ottawa, where they met Prime Minister Wilfrid Laurier, and then by ship to England to present their grievances to King Edward VII. They met with the king and returned to British Columbia hoping their voices had been heard. This trip showed that BC First Nations were taking the struggle for Aboriginal rights into their own hands.

Continued on next page

Top: Su-a-pu-luck (fifth from left, front row) gathers on the North Vancouver ferry wharf in May 1908 with a delegation of Coast Salish leaders as they prepare to leave for a second meeting with Prime Minister Wilfrid Laurier. NVMA 957

Right: Joe Capilano in 1908, the year he made another trip east, this time only as far as Ottawa, with a delegation of other First Nations leaders. NVMA 2849

Joe Capilano died in 1910. His wife, Mary Agnes, who lived until 1940, was a noted storyteller and genealogist. Chief Simon Baker, her grandson, recalled how she used to paddle her canoe across to Vancouver to sell produce door-to-door: "I remember she used to go in her dugout canoe from the Capilano Reserve across the narrows into Vancouver where the old Immigration Building used to be. She'd tie up there and pack her clams, berries, baskets and mats to the Hotel Vancouver and around the West End where all the rich people lived—the Rogers, MacMillans, McDermids, Bell-Irvings—all those people used to ask my grandmother to bring them fresh berries and clams."[7]

Left: Mary Agnes Capilano in 1939, the year before her death. CVA Port 430

Above: Basket maker Sophie Frank (bottom left) and her family. Emily Carr met Sophie Frank in 1906 and they remained friends until Frank's death in 1939. Carr devoted a chapter of her book *Klee Wyck* to Frank. NVMA 7120

These First Nations baskets are from the collection of the North Vancouver Museum and Archives. Squamish girls learned to weave baskets from an early age. Made from spruce root, cedar bark and other plant material, baskets were used as containers by the First Nations. After the arrival of Europeans, baskets became items of trade and sale as well. NVMA photos

Above: This octagonal wicker plaited basket with lid is attributed to Mary Capilano. NVMA 1980.60.1

Above: A Squamish cedar root tray with decoration in red cherry bark, black-dyed cherry bark and white grass. It is attributed to Melina Moody. NVMA 1980.60.1

Ferries and Bridges

With the North Shore waterfront filling in, settlers felt the pressing need for reliable transportation between the different communities on the inlet. John ("Navvy Jack") Thomas, a pioneer settler in West Vancouver, inaugurated the first "ferry" in 1866 when he began using his 9-metre sailing sloop to offer unscheduled service between New Brighton, where the road to New Westminster began, Moodyville and the Hastings Mill. Thomas would also row passengers across the inlet for a price. Two years later Captain James van Bramer, one of Sewell Moody's original partners in the sawmill, initiated a more formal service between the same three points with his small steam tug, *Sea Foam*. At Brighton, on the south side of the Second Narrows, there was a hotel where travellers could connect with the stagecoach service to New Westminster. *Sea Foam* was the first of several vessels employed by the enterprising Captain van Bramer. The most eccentric member of his fleet was the *Union*, which was little more than an open scow with a threshing machine engine powering two paddlewheels. It had no reverse gear and lost power whenever its whistle sounded, so passengers had to brace themselves against its herky-jerky motion (doubtless the reason the *Union* was more commonly called the *Sudden Jerk*). In 1881 a new steam ferry made its appearance. Built by the Moodyville Ferry Company, the *Senator* was 16 metres in length and sometimes towed a scow to carry wagons and livestock. Passengers paid ten cents to cross the inlet.

In 1889 a group of Vancouver business interests created a new steamship company to provide regular service to the small camps and settlements that were appearing along the length of the BC coast. The Union Steamship Company, as it was called, would grow to become the north coast's main lifeline to the outside world for over half a century. In its infancy it acquired the *Senator* and used it to maintain the triangular ferry route between Moodyville and the south shore of the inlet. When the residents of North Vancouver decided it was time to connect their new commercial centre at the bottom of Lonsdale Avenue with the rising metropolis across the inlet, they invited the Union Steamship Company to include their community in the *Senator*'s regular run.

"My father was returning from the City on the usual evening trip [on the *Senator*] and was standing on the small deck with his back to the low railing which came to about knee level. The skipper made a poor landing and struck the wharf quite sharply with the result that my father went over backwards into the cold waters of the Inlet. Fortunately he was an excellent swimmer as he carried the usual rucksack on his back packed with groceries and held a can of milk in his hand. He swam around the wharf to the rocky shoreline and clambered safely ashore, much to the astonishment of the crew and passengers who had conducted a search for him. He not only survived the cold swim but came ashore with the rucksack and canned milk still tightly grasped in his hand. He then faced a mile climb up the hill to 15th Street where his homestead was located."

—Thomas Diplock, unpublished memoir, 1978[8]

Top: The steam ferry *Senator* boarding passengers in Vancouver, ca. 1890, for the crossing to Moodyville. It was named for Senator Hugh Nelson, one of Sewell Moody's partners in the mill. NVMA 280

Bottom: Two ferries at the wharf at the foot of Lonsdale Avenue. Note the horse-drawn wagons loading on the left, and the crowds of passengers boarding for the commute across to Vancouver. NVMA 3222

A view of Lonsdale Avenue at about the time the city formed a separate municipality. Streetcars are trundling up the hill and Lower Lonsdale has emerged as the business centre of the North Shore. NVMA 457

HARDWARE
LUMBER & SHINGLES
WESTERN CORPORATION LTD
AUCTIONEERS HOUSE FURNISHERS
REAL ESTATE AGENTS. SECRETARIES. BROKERS.

For many decades boats from the Cates fleet were a recognizable symbol of the Vancouver harbour. NVMA 798

This still left West Vancouver isolated without ferry service. In 1899 Captain John Cates—brother of Charles Henry Cates, the founder of C. H. Cates & Sons towing—began his own company, the Terminal Steamship Company. He used his vessels to run regular freight and passenger service to Bowen Island, Howe Sound and Indian Arm. They would stop along the shore outside the First Narrows if a red flag was raised as a signal. Early in 1910 the West Vancouver Transportation Company launched a regular ferry between a wharf at the foot of 17th Street and downtown Vancouver, using a converted fishboat renamed the *West Vancouver No. 1*. Two years later the newly formed municipality took over the service, shifting its headquarters to a new ferry building at the foot of 14th Street (a building that today contains a community art gallery).

Meanwhile, North Vancouver commuters grew impatient with the irregular service being offered by the Union Steamship Company. In 1900 the District decided to take matters into its own hands; it built a new ferry, the *North Vancouver*, and took over the service itself. The problem was that, when it came time to expand, local government did not have the necessary resources to build another, larger vessel. At this point, real estate developer

Top: The District-owned *North Vancouver* approaches the dock at the foot of Lonsdale Avenue, ca. 1901. NVMA 198

Bottom: *North Vancouver Ferry #4* on one of its last sailings. The ferry to North Vancouver ceased operating in 1958. NVMA 11361

Alfred St. George Hamersley stepped in. He had subdivided a large chunk of Lower Lonsdale, but if buyers were going to settle there, they needed to be assured of a reliable commute to Vancouver. Hamersley and some partners incorporated the North Vancouver Ferry and Power Company and assumed control of the ferry service. Their new vessel, the *St. George*, began operation in mid-1904. It was double-ended, with capacity for a thousand passengers and up to fourteen wagons with their teams of horses. When the City incorporated in 1907, it created the North Vancouver City Ferries Ltd., and the ferries returned to public ownership, where they remained for the next fifty years. The *St. George* was rechristened *North Vancouver #2* and each new vessel as it joined the fleet became #3, #4, and so on. Passengers

This is a scale model of the *Charles H. Cates XV*, a 1950s-era wooden tug belonging to the Cates fleet. The model was made in 1990 by Ian Cunningham. NVMA 2013.1.1 Shawn McDonald photo

A WATERFRONT FAMILY

Beginning in the 1880s, Charles Henry Cates used his fleet of tugboats to haul building supplies and to tow barges and other vessels around the Vancouver harbour. Eventually he was joined in the business by three sons, all of whom were certified sea captains. The company they formed, C. H. Cates and Sons (later Cates Towing), based at the foot of Lonsdale Avenue, was a fixture on the Burrard Inlet waterfront. One son served as a member of the provincial legislature; another son was a mayor of North Vancouver City, as was daughter-in-law Carrie Cates, the first woman elected to the position. The towboat operation endures as part of the Seaspan group of companies.

came and went from the wharf at the foot of Lonsdale where, in the early years, a one-armed Chilean immigrant named Joe Bustamante—he had lost his limb in a mill accident—blew his trumpet to guide the ferry through the fog to its berth. Every day, residents of both the City and the District crossed the water to and from their jobs in downtown Vancouver or to shop in the stores along Hastings Street. After initially floundering, the municipal ferry company prospered during World War I and by 1921 it was transporting more than a quarter million passengers each month. When *North Vancouver #4* joined the service in 1931, it had capacity to carry twenty-six automobiles.

During the Depression the ferry service struggled, along with every other business on the North Shore. But in addition to the usual strains of the economic downturn, the ferries were coping with competition from an alternative means of crossing the inlet: bridges. A bridge across the inlet had first been raised in 1892 when the Burrard Inlet Tunnel and Bridge Company announced plans to build both a bridge and a tunnel across the First Narrows. The tunnel never materialized but the bridge was the subject of negotiation and debate for many years, until finally the increased use of automobiles during the 1920s brought pressure on local governments to move forward with the project. With financial

The Second Narrows Bridge in 1925, shortly after its completion. NVMA 748

support from all levels of government, the company constructed a wooden trestle bridge across the Second Narrows to a point on the North Shore just to the west of Seymour Creek. A rail line occupied the centre of the bridge, flanked on each side by a lane of car traffic. A lift span was located at the south end, allowing ship traffic access to the inner inlet.

When the Second Narrows Bridge opened on November 7, 1925, it was the first automobile and rail link between the north and south shores. Unfortunately, in order to save money the designers of the bridge had placed the lift span too close to the shallow side of the narrows and vessels routinely struck the piers, putting the crossing out of commission for various lengths of time. Finally, in September 1930, a log barge became wedged under the centre span and a rising tide forced the barge up against the underside of the bridge, dislodging the span. It was the Depression and the municipalities could not afford to fix it, so the "Bridge of Sighs," as it had become known, remained closed for four long years, cutting North Vancouver off from road access and requiring railway companies to barge their cars across.

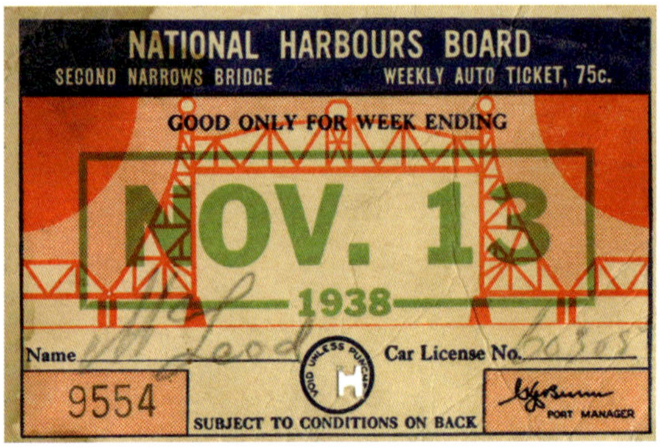

NVMA Item 965

To residents of the North Shore, the

The original Second Narrows Bridge, which opened in 1925, was so prone to mishap that it was known derisively as the Bridge of Sighs. NVMA 4403

lesson was obvious: a second crossing should be built at the First Narrows. The idea had been discussed for several years, but because it required an access road through Stanley Park, Vancouver residents had not been enthusiastic. With the arrival of the Depression, minds changed. Building a bridge and causeway suddenly became attractive ways to provide much-needed jobs for the unemployed. The closure of the Second Narrows crossing gave added incentive to the project. In a 1933 plebiscite, Vancouver voters overwhelmingly endorsed the bridge and causeway. While the Depression had provided the rationale for a second bridge, it also left local governments unable to pay for it. Which is why the bridge at the First Narrows, unlike the Second Narrows crossing, was financed completely by private capital from a syndicate organized by Vancouver engineer and entrepreneur A. J. T. "Fred" Taylor. The syndicate, dominated by the Guinness brewing family, desired a bridge in order to improve access to its real estate holdings in West Vancouver. Construction got underway in the spring of 1937, and the Lions Gate Bridge opened

Construction of the Lions Gate Bridge required the erection of two towers, between which bundles of steel cable were strung across the narrows. This photograph shows the progress made by mid-May 1938. NVMA 363

Clockwise from top left: One of the workers poses atop a bundle of cable strands during Lions Gate Bridge construction (NVMA 1156.4)**. The steel roadbed was suspended in sections from the steel cables high above** (NVMA 1156.02)**. The south entrance to the bridge from the causeway** (NVMA 1156.12)**.**

to two lanes of automobile traffic on November 14, 1938. Initially it was a toll bridge: pedestrians and bicyclists paid five cents to cross, while a car and driver cost twenty-five cents (each passenger was an extra nickel). At the beginning of 1955, the provincial government took over ownership of the bridge, and on April 1, 1963, once the province had recouped the six million dollars it had paid, the tolls were removed. By then, two lanes had become three and millions of vehicles crossed the span each year.

The bridge across the First Narrows was built mainly to serve West Vancouver, but its impact on North Vancouver was profound as well. Suddenly the western side of the District was accessible by automobile as never before, stimulating unprecedented residential and commercial development, especially once World War II was over. With the Second Narrows Bridge back in operation from 1934, North Vancouver emerged from the Depression and the war with two dependable road connections to the rest of the Lower Mainland and a bright future as a residential suburb of Vancouver, and ultimately an urban centre in its own right.

Every silver lining has a cloud, however. The publicly owned ferry system prospered during World War II, when the booming shipbuilding industry on the North Shore brought a daily influx of thousands of workers across the inlet. Following the war, however, the ferries fell on hard times. Residents of the burgeoning residential neighbourhoods in the District preferred the convenience of their own automobiles, so the bridges were siphoning away

Top: A colour postcard shows the completed Lions Gate Bridge with the two lions, sculpted by local artist Charles Marega. NVMA 1939-5

Above: A car window sticker for the new bridge. NVMA 966-2

customers from the ferry. The last North Vancouver ferry made its final run on August 30, 1958.

For the next twenty years, North Vancouverites had no ferry connection across Burrard Inlet. The bridges expanded to handle the increased volume of commuter traffic. At the Second Narrows, the old bridge proved inadequate to the demands of the postwar North Vancouver expansion. It still had only two lanes and a lift span that stopped car and rail traffic every time a deep-sea vessel passed through. In 1956 construction began on a replacement, a six-lane high level span that, when completed, would be the eighth-longest cantilever bridge in the world. Tragically, the site continued to be cursed. On June 17, 1958, the partially completed

The collapse of the second Second Narrows Bridge while under construction in June 1958 claimed twenty-four lives. Blame for the collapse was attributed to engineering error. NVMA 9940

span collapsed into the water with a giant roar. A total of twenty-four people died: eighteen workers and engineers in the initial collapse, five of injuries, and a diver who was killed searching for bodies. An inquiry blamed the catastrophe on a mistake made by two of the engineers who died. Construction resumed and the new bridge opened in August 1960. (In 1994 it was renamed Ironworkers Memorial Second Narrows Crossing in remembrance of the terrible accident.)

Year by year, traffic increased on the bridges as the population of the District grew. Demands from harried drivers for some sort of "third crossing" grew more insistent. Finally, in June 1977, the provincial government reached into the past and reinstituted the Burrard Inlet ferry in modern dress. SeaBus was a new, passenger-only commuter service between floating terminals at the Lonsdale Quay at the foot of Lonsdale Avenue and the former Canadian Pacific Railway station on the Vancouver waterfront. The double-ended, catamaran style SeaBus vessels scoot across the inlet in just twelve minutes and are totally integrated with the North Vancouver bus service. The new ferry added to the economic revitalization of the Lower Lonsdale area, but also gave District residents who wanted to park their cars an alternative way of getting to Vancouver. Today SeaBus vessels carry more than six million passengers a year across Burrard Inlet.

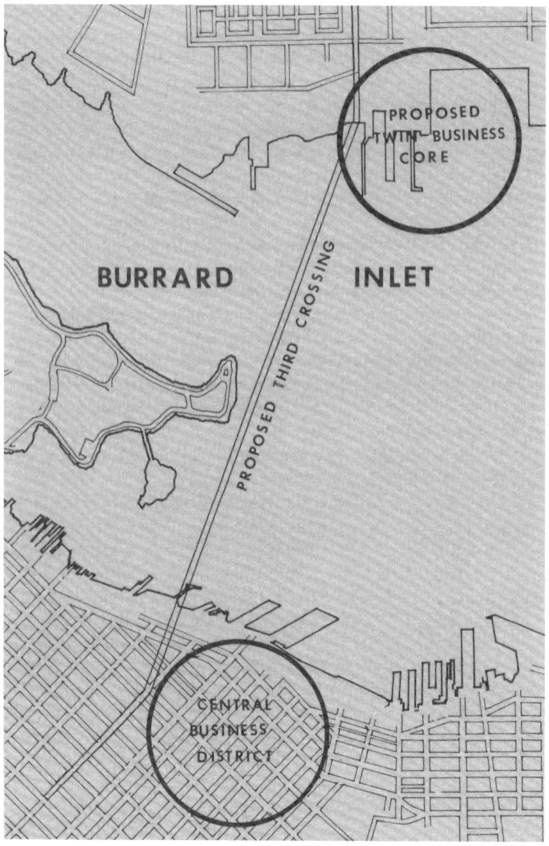

A 1974 vision of a possible Third Crossing, a combination bridge and tunnel.
NVMA NA9130.V2 K455 (1)

A THIRD CROSSING

With the increase in automobile traffic, the idea of another bridge or tunnel linking the North Shore and downtown Vancouver was much debated during the 1960s. Ideas ranged from "twinning" the Lions Gate crossing to a tunnel beneath the inlet to a new, six-lane bridge at Brockton Point. Plans also included a complex new freeway system for the Vancouver waterfront. In the end, opposition to such large-scale redevelopment prevailed and plans were dropped in favour of improved public transit.

It was back to the future when the SeaBus passenger ferry between North Vancouver and downtown Vancouver began service in 1977. NVMA 12754

The Shipbuilding Industry

North Vancouver's first export industry was sawmilling. In November 1864 the barque *Ellen Lewis* set sail from the Moodyville dock carrying a huge load of lumber, rail ties and pickets bound for Australia, inaugurating the port of Vancouver. Twenty years later, writes historian James Delgado, "the mills of Burrard Inlet [Moodyville among them] exported 24 million board feet of rough lumber, 2.2 million feet of milled lumber and a million feet of pickets in forty-three vessels."[9] The Moodyville mill closed in 1901 but it was followed by several other mills producing wood products for foreign markets. Among the largest of these were Robert Dollar's mill, established near Roche Point in 1916; the Capilano Timber Company's mill, which operated at the foot of Pemberton Avenue from 1919 until it was destroyed by fire in 1932; and the M. B. King Lumber Company mill, established at the foot of Fell Avenue in 1933. Air pollution from the mills contributed to the acrid fogs that used to smother the Lower Mainland. Sawdust-burning home furnaces, steam railway engines, beehive burners at the sawmills: all contributed to a high percentage of particulate matter in the air, which led to dense fogs that made driving hazardous and the air unhealthy. Quite commonly the view across the inlet was obscured by the haze. This situation improved as home heating systems converted to oil and natural gas, and industrial pollutants decreased. Today, when the fog does occur, it is due to weather conditions, not industry.

A painting of the *Ellen Lewis* by North Vancouver artist and cartoonist David Alavoine. The vessel sailed from Moodyville in November 1864, bound for Australia, carrying the first foreign shipment of lumber out of Burrard Inlet. NVMA David Alavoine Fonds 185

The M.B. King lumber mill at the foot of Fell Avenue, in operation from 1933 to 1972, was one of the major industrial sites on the waterfront. NVMA 7568

Top: Horne Brothers was one of the sawmills on the North Vancouver waterfront. Located just west of what is now the Lonsdale Quay, it was in operation from the 1920s to the 1980s. NVMA 6075

Bottom: Sign for Horne Brothers Shingle Company. NVMA 1981.81.1

Top: Men erecting the wooden ribs of one of the wooden schooners at Wallace Shipyards #2, July 1916. NVMA 4924

Bottom: The men who built the ships pose at the Wallace yards between the two world wars. NVMA 27-713

Right: Betty Brown, daughter of the owner of the shipping company for which the Mabel Brown class of vessels were built, launches the first of the series at the Wallace yard, 1917. VPL 20099

350.

early the next year. At the same time, the government contracted for three steel-hulled freighters—*War Dog*, the first steel ocean-going vessel built in Canada, *War Power* and *War Storm*—each 96 metres (315 ft) long with 1,300 horsepower steam engines. So much construction required an expansion of the initial shipyard and the addition of a second plant, Shipyard #2, at the foot of Bewicke Avenue on the so-called "Fell fill" site. (The Fell site was originally owned by land developer James P. Fell, who filled in the tidal flats in 1912 for a planned deepwater docking facility. When the war interrupted these plans, the shipyard located on the property.) Wallace Shipyards, which began the war with 172 employees, had more than 1,000 before it was over. Most of these workers commuted by ferry from across the inlet, but many lived in the City and District.

With the end of the war, business fell off. Shipyard #2 was sold and became Lyall Shipyards. Wallace replaced military contracts with domestic vessels, and most of its business was repair and refitting. Chief among the new vessels was the *Princess Louise*, a 97-metre (318 ft) steel ship built for the CPR's Princess Line of elegant coastal steamers. Launched in August 1921, the

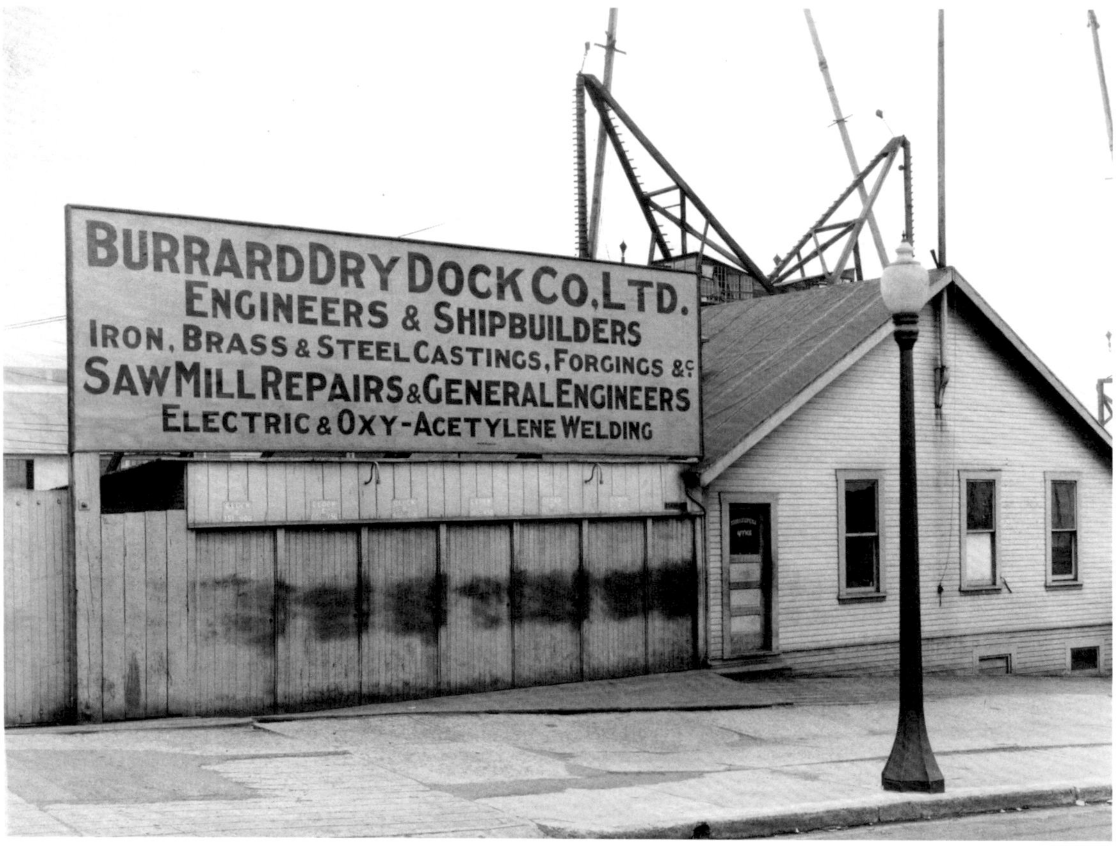

Above: The timekeeper's office in 1928, shortly after Wallace Shipyards became the Burrard Dry Dock Company. NVMA 12842

Right: The *Princess Louise* on the slipway at Wallace Shipyards prior to its launch in 1921. NVMA 2045

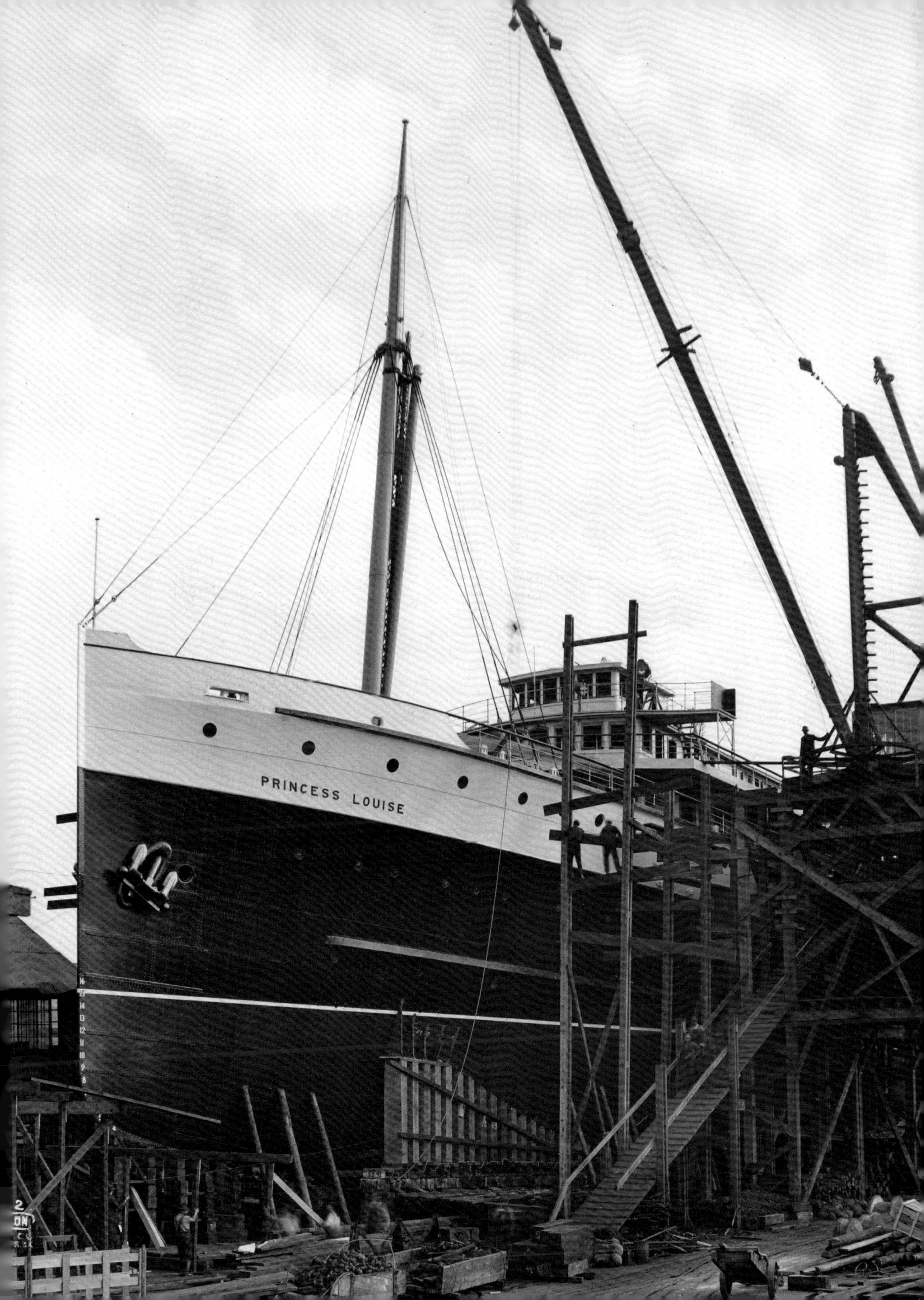
PRINCESS LOUISE

Louise, which remained in operation until 1962, was the largest passenger vessel built in the province up to that time. The quality of the workmanship showed that locally made ships could be every bit as good as those manufactured in Great Britain. Not long after its completion, Wallace Shipyards became the Burrard Dry Dock Company with the addition of a floating dry dock where large, ocean-going vessels could be repaired, the first of its kind on the Pacific coast.

THE *ST. ROCH*

One of the most famous vessels to emerge from the Wallace Shipyards during the interwar period was the *St. Roch*. Built for the Royal Canadian Mounted Police (RCMP) to patrol the High Arctic, the *St. Roch* was made of thick Douglas fir planks reinforced with heavy beams to absorb the pressure of the ice pack. It was launched in North Vancouver in 1928 and remained in service for a quarter of a century, carrying supplies into the North and serving as a floating police detachment. Most famously, the *St. Roch* was the first vessel to navigate the Northwest Passage through the Arctic from west to east (1940–42), spending two winters trapped in the ice. Then it turned around and completed the same trip in the opposite direction in a single season, again for the first time. To top things off, after retiring from the Arctic in 1950 it became the first vessel to circumnavigate North America.

The *St. Roch*, a National Historic Site, is on display at the Vancouver Maritime Museum, not many kilometres from its birthplace on the North Vancouver waterfront.

Finishing touches being applied to the *St. Roch* on the North Vancouver waterfront, 1928. NVMA 27-2458

Allied Shipbuilders Ltd., located east of the Ironworkers Memorial bridge, has been a major industrial employer on the North Shore for about seventy years. NVMA 160-64. Bruce Flanagan photo

NORTH VANCOUVER'S "OTHER" SHIPYARD

Allied Shipbuilders Ltd. Is another important shipyard on the North Vancouver waterfront. It was established by Arthur McLaren in 1948 near the mouth of the Seymour River and remains in operation today. Allied has built almost three hundred vessels over the years, from fishboats to barges, tugs and icebreakers. For almost sixty-five years the company was owned and managed by members of the McLaren family, until they sold their controlling interest to a long-time employee in 2012.

With the outbreak of World War II, the demand by Allied countries for naval vessels made North Vancouver crucially important to the war effort. The Burrard Dry Dock Company and North Van Ship Repair were among the six British Columbia yards capable of building the large vessels demanded by Great Britain, whose own yards could not keep up due to the losses being inflicted by German submarines. North Vancouver's two shipyards produced nearly half of the vessels, both military and cargo, manufactured in Canada during the war. It was a remarkable achievement for such a small community. Burrard Dry Dock was so busy that it had to open another yard, Burrard South, across the inlet on the Vancouver waterfront.

With the end of the war, the shipbuilding boom was over. The Burrard Dry Dock Company closed its Burrard South yard and, in 1951, purchased North Van Ship

Repair, which it promptly closed down. The main facility continued in operation, building and repairing a variety of vessels: coastal ferries, naval and Coast Guard ships, barges and tugs. But by the 1970s the Canadian shipbuilding industry had become uncompetitive internationally and the federal government was not going to subsidize it by ordering new vessels. In

Above: This painting, titled *Organization*, depicts a night scene at Burrard Dry Dock in 1944 when union organizers were prevented from entering the shipyard. The artist was Fraser Wilson, who had worked in the yard as a young man. NVMA 2012.17.1

Right: End of shift and the wartime workers at Burrard Dry Dock flood out onto Lonsdale Avenue to catch the ferry across the inlet. NVMA 27-679

1972 the Wallace family, which had owned the company from the beginning, sold Burrard Dry Dock to Cornat Industries, part of the Canadian Forest Products empire. In 1985, it was renamed Versatile Pacific Shipyards. At the end of 1992 the shipyard shut down, leaving only the dry dock in operation. Today much of the old shipyard site is being redeveloped as a historic district and public gathering spot.

But shipbuilding on the North Shore is not dead, far from it. Today Vancouver Drydock, which is owned by Seaspan, continues to carry out maintenance and repairs to a wide variety of vessels, while Vancouver Shipyards, also owned by Seaspan and located at the foot of Pemberton Avenue, has been newly

Above: This brass bell, mounted on the Pacific Great Eastern train, warned of oncoming rail traffic. NVMA 1984.84 Shawn McDonald photo

modernized to accommodate large construction projects, including the addition of Canada's largest gantry crane. During the 1990s Vancouver Shipyards participated in the construction of three "PacifiCat" aluminum ferries for the BC Ferries. While these speedy catamaran vessels proved to be unsuited to coastal routes and had to be sold, their construction was nonetheless a notable milestone for shipbuilding on the North Shore. In 2011 the industry received a tremendous shot in the arm when Seaspan received a multi-billion dollar federal government contract to construct several vessels for the Canadian Coast Guard and the Royal Canadian Navy.

THE NORTH SHORE'S OWN RAILWAY

Prior to the outbreak of World War I, North Vancouverites came down with a serious case of railway fever. In the heady prewar years of economic expansion, a rail link between the Lower Mainland and the central interior of the province via Howe Sound and Squamish seemed like a possible dream rather than the financial nightmare it became. Incorporated in 1912 using capital mainly raised in Great Britain, the Pacific Great Eastern Railway (PGE) was planned to run north to Prince George, a distance of 735 kilometres, where it would intersect with the transcontinental Grand Trunk Pacific line then being completed to the Pacific at Prince Rupert.

Eventually, optimists predicted, the PGE would extend all the way to the Peace River area and draw down all the resources of the Interior to the port at Burrard Inlet. In the short term, however, these plans were thwarted by the prewar end to the economic boom and the difficulty of laying track along the steep shores of Howe Sound. Still, the company did manage to complete a short (20-kilometre) commuter line along the North Shore waterfront, between a terminal at Lonsdale Avenue and Whytecliff in West Vancouver. Known as the "North Shore Subdivision," it began regular passenger service all the way to Whytecliff in the summer of 1914.

Continued on pg 62

Opposite and above: The North Shore Subdivision of the Pacific Great Eastern makes its inaugural run, January 1, 1914. For the first six months the passenger service ran only as far as Dundarave in West Vancouver. Opposite: NVMA 2014; above: NVMA 10746

Pacific Great Eastern Railway

NOTICE

Passengers desirous of boarding trains must stand in view of approaching train and signal engineer to stop.

Above and right: There were fifteen stations on the North Shore line between Lonsdale Avenue and Whytecliff. NVMA photos

PACIFIC GREAT EASTERN RAILWAY

CONSTRUCTION DEPARTMENT

TIME TABLE NUMBER 7

TAKING EFFECT 12.01 A.M. SUNDAY, DECEMBER 27TH, 1914

SUBJECT TO CHANGE WITHOUT NOTICE — GOVERNED BY PACIFIC TIME

WESTBOUND TRAINS First Class							Miles from N. Vancouver	STATIONS	Station Numbers	EASTBOUND TRAINS First Class					
14 Daily P.M.	12 Daily P.M.	10 Daily P.M.	8 Daily P.M.	6 Daily A.M.	4 Daily A.M.	2 Daily A.M.				3 Daily A.M.	5 Daily A.M.	7 Daily P.M.	9 Daily P.M.	11 Daily P.M.	13 Daily P.M.
7.20	5.40	3.40	1.40	10.40	8.40			s NORTH VANCOUVER	A	8.17	10.17	12.17	3.17	5.17	7.17
							.8	f FELL STREET	B						
							1.7	f PEMBERTON AVE.	C						
7.27	5.47	3.47	1.47	10.47	8.47		2.4	f CAPILANO	D	8.10	10.10	12.10	3.10	5.10	7.10
7.31	5.51	3.51	1.51	10.51	8.51		3.7	f AMBLESIDE	E	8.06	10.06	12.06	3.06	5.06	7.06
7.33	5.53	3.53	1.53	10.53	8.53		4.0	f HOLLYBURN	F	8.04	10.04	12.04	3.04	5.04	7.04
7.35	5.55	3.55	1.55	10.55	8.55		4.5	f WESTON	G	8.01	10.01	12.01	3.01	5.01	7.01
7.37	5.57	3.57	1.57	10.57	8.57		5.2	s DUNDARAVE	H	7.58	9.58	11.58	2.58	4.58	6.58
7.40	6.00	4.00	2.00	11.00	9.00	a.m. 7.00	5.7	s ALTAMONT	I	7.56	9.56	11.56	2.56	4.56	6.56
							6.7	f WESTBAY	J						
	6.08	4.08	2.08	11.08	9.08	7.08	8.2	f CYPRESS PARK	L	7.44	9.44	11.44	2.44	4.44	6.44
	6.11	4.11	2.11	11.11	9.11	7.11	8.7	f CAULFEILD	N	7.42	9.42	11.42	2.42	4.42	6.42
	6.15	4.15	2.15	11.15	9.15	7.15	10.1	f EAGLE HARBOR	P	7.38	9.38	11.38	2.38	4.38	6.38
	6.23	4.23	2.23	11.23	9.23	7.23	12.3	f LARSONS	R	7.31	9.31	11.31	2.31	4.31	6.31
p.m.	6.25 p.m.	4.25 p.m.	2.25 p.m.	11.25 a.m.	9.25 a.m.	7.25 a.m.	12.7	s WHYTECLIFF	S	7.30 a.m.	9.30 a.m.	11.30 a.m.	2.30 p.m.	4.30 p.m.	6.30 p.m.

A man's knitted wool sweater displaying the Pacific Great Eastern logo and the names of the stations along the route to the Interior. The sweater was knit by Jack Sommers, a section foreman on the line. It sold for $35 in 1958.
NVMA 1991.27.1 Shawn McDonald photo

For the next fourteen years the dark red, gasoline-powered cars of the North Shore line carried commuters on several runs a day to their residences in North and West Vancouver, along with recreationists heading for the beaches and picnic grounds at Horseshoe Bay and Whytecliff. The line was plagued by difficulties, especially in the winter and spring when heavy rains and runoff regularly damaged the trestles and bridges that carried the track across the Capilano River and the many creeks and streams flowing down off the mountains. In the end, as the anticipated freight business from the Interior did not materialize, it became too expensive to maintain a small passenger line in the face of growing competition from automobiles and buses, and on November 29, 1928, the North Shore line closed.

More than a quarter century later, the North Shore Subdivision got a second life. The PGE had continued its on-again, off-again progress toward the interior. In 1952 the line between Squamish and Prince George finally opened and, four years later, track was laid along the shore of Howe Sound to Whytecliff. As a result the moribund line into North Vancouver was resurrected and train service between North Vancouver and the interior of the province became a reality. Today passenger service has been discontinued but the line, later operated by BC Rail and now by CN Rail, continues to carry freight traffic to the Interior.

North Vancouver and the Port

The arrival of the railway in Vancouver was the most important development in the emergence of Burrard Inlet as a global port. Without the railways, first the Canadian Pacific in 1886, then several other transcontinental lines, the inlet would not have been transformed into a transhipment point for goods heading into and out of North America, goods such as grain from the Canadian Prairies, coal and other minerals from the BC Interior and rice, tea and silk from Asia. Because of its rail links, Burrard Inlet (including the North Shore) became Canada's gateway to the Pacific world.

Initial developments in the port were concentrated on the Vancouver side of the inlet. The full involvement of North Vancouver in the growing trans-Pacific trade was delayed until the construction of the Second Narrows Bridge in the mid-

Sawmilling once played a vital part in the North Vancouver industrial economy. The Lions Gate Lumber Company operated this mill at the foot of Lloyd Avenue, seen ca. 1950. NVMA 537

Top: Forest-based industry once dominated the North Vancouver waterfront. These barges were loading with sawdust at the L & K Lumber Co. dock at the foot of Phillip Avenue in 1979. NVMA 160-149. Bruce Flanagan photo

Above: The Midland Pacific grain terminals were built in 1928 and 1929 on fill land just east of the site of Moodyville. NVMA 3349

This aerial view of log booms on the waterfront in 1927 illustrates the importance of the forest industry to the inter-war economy of North Vancouver. NVMA 5560

Vancouver Wharves, shown here in 1969, is a bulk product terminal, part of the post–World War II expansion that transformed the Industrial waterfront of North Vancouver.
NVMA 11203

1920s brought rail access to the North Shore. Dirt from the Moodyville hillside was used to fill in the tidal flats west of the bridge, creating several hectares of reclaimed foreshore that was used by the rail line and for commercial purposes, including the first grain export terminal on the North Shore, built by the Midland Pacific company in 1928. The opening of the Panama Canal during World War I had made it possible to ship Canadian grain to Europe via Vancouver's port. During the 1920s the volume of this trade increased dramatically and the success of the Midland Pacific elevator led to construction the following year of an expansion that tripled its capacity. (This terminal has been owned by Richardson International, alone or in partnership, since 1954.)

> "Talking about the North Shore. We always went over by ferry. Very few men had cars in those days and even if they did have there was no way of getting over except by ferry. When you did get over to the North Shore it was a good mile walk from the foot of Lonsdale to the Midland Pacific. So you can imagine how many times we have arrived at the Midland soaking wet and then having to go down in the dusty wheat and what it felt like finishing at night. Maybe 9 or 10 o'clock and coming up and walking back to the ferry and it would still be pouring. Getting on the ferry and getting home. . . . But what I have to say about getting over to the North Shore is that it cost a nickel to get through the turnstile. I can remember many a time, being small, getting a piggy-back on top of a guy's shoulders and both of us going through the turnstile for one nickel."
> —Longshoreman Alex Will[10]

Seaspan barges being loaded with sawdust, 1979.
NVMA 160-150. Bruce Flanagan photo

The closure of the Second Narrows Bridge in the early 1930s, not to mention the economic downturn of the Depression, created a hiccup in waterfront development but the pace resumed later in the decade with the creation by the federal government of a new agency to manage major ports across Canada, including Vancouver's harbour. With port traffic increasing, the National Harbours Board encouraged the reclamation of more tidal areas for industrial purposes. Along the North Vancouver shore this resulted in the

The iconic sulphur piles at the Vancouver Wharves terminal east of the Lions Gate Bridge are a symbol of the North Vancouver waterfront, September 1979.
NVMA 183-237. Bruce Flanagan photo

A view across the waterfront industrial area to the Ironworkers Memorial bridge.
NVMA 106-26-4

creation of many hectares of new land for use as deepwater terminal facilities. For example, Vancouver Wharves, a bulk product terminal across from Stanley Park, stands out for its glowing piles of yellow sulphur. Opened in 1959, Vancouver Wharves is now owned by Kinder Morgan. Next door is the Fibreco terminal, created by a consortium of sawmill companies in 1977 to export wood chips and wood pellets for the world pulp and paper industry. The National Harbours Board constructed another bulk terminal, Neptune Terminals, to the west of Lynn Creek near the old Moodyville site. When it opened in 1968, it was the largest multi-product bulk terminal in North America, handling potash, coal, fertilizers and other products.

All of these port-related facilities, and several others, occupy land recovered from the tidal flats that once lined the north shore of the harbour. Once upon a time the entire shoreline consisted of mud flats where the First Nations gathered shellfish and hunted waterfowl. With the construction of the railway tracks, the shipyards and the shipping terminals, this original shoreline was filled in and extended out into the harbour. In total, 80 percent of the original shoreline of Burrard Inlet's inner harbour, north shore and south, has been altered over the years by port-related activities, resulting in the loss of almost 53 kilometres of natural shoreline. This industrial expansion has devastated the populations of fish and waterfowl that use the streams for spawning and wetlands for feeding. It has destroyed habitat, polluted waterways with industrial effluent and disrupted the natural life cycle of many animal species. Logging on the mountain slopes removed thousands of hectares of forest, fouling the rivers and streams with detritus and increasing water runoff, which in turn caused damaging floods. It

The *Clifford J. Rogers*, the world's first purpose-built container ship, sailed from North Vancouver on its inaugural voyage at the end of 1955. This photograph shows cars sitting on top of the containers. NVMA 10748

is difficult to calculate just how profoundly industrial development has altered the natural environment of the North Shore.

Along with its bulk freight terminals, North Vancouver also pioneered the use of containers to transship goods between seagoing carriers and land-based trucks and rail. Back in 1955, containers were an untested technology; the *Clifford J. Rogers*, the world's first purpose-built container ship, was a 101-metre (336-ft) freighter constructed in Montreal and delivered to Vancouver in the fall of that year. It carried six hundred cube-shaped steel containers for the White Pass & Yukon Route from its North Vancouver terminal to Skagway, Alaska, where the goods were lifted aboard the railway and hauled to Whitehorse. The experiment proved to be the beginning of a transportation revolution. In 2014 Port

Lowering containers into the hold of the *Clifford J. Rogers* at its North Vancouver berth. NVMA 9626 image 1

Metro Vancouver handled almost three million container-loads of cargo at four container facilities, and the giant red gantry cranes that shift the containers have become a fixture of the Vancouver skyline.

"Very few people are aware that many of the most commonly used underwater tools or technologies used all over the world were invented in Canada. For some reason Canada, and particularly western Canada, has been an absolute hotbed of submarine design and development. And that came about as a result of a company here called 'International Hydrodynamics' that existed in North Vancouver. And they developed a world-class submersible long, long before anyone was building them on a routine basis. . . . They were so successful that they drew underwater technologists and engineers from all over the world to work here in North Vancouver."
—Phil Nyutten, inventor and deepwater exploration pioneer

Today the Port of Vancouver is Canada's largest port, handling more than 140 million tonnes of cargo worth $187 billion in 2014. The North Shore Trade Area (NSTA) consists of the port terminals and industrial activity along the North Vancouver waterfront between the two bridges. With its bulk terminals, chemical plants and grain elevators, the NSTA contributes a significant portion of the port's trade. Major commodities include coal, potash, sulphur, chemicals, agri-products and forest products. In general the NSTA handles about 35 percent of all cargo volume through the Port of Vancouver.

The North Shore waterfront has come a long way since the first few loads of lumber left the Moodyville docks bound for the trans-Pacific trade a century and a half ago. It is now one of the most heavily industrialized areas in the Lower Mainland. Logging, sawmilling, shipbuilding and deep-sea shipping together laid the economic foundation. But that is only part of the story of North Vancouver. At the same time as industry filled the waterfront, a vibrant community was taking shape across the lower slopes of the North Shore Mountains. Initially a suburb of Vancouver, this community with its head in the clouds and its feet in the waters of Burrard Inlet grew to become a prosperous, lively and diverse urban centre in its own right.

The North Vancouver working waterfront handles 35 percent of the cargo flowing through the Port of Vancouver. Lisa Wilson photo

BUILDING COMMUNITIES

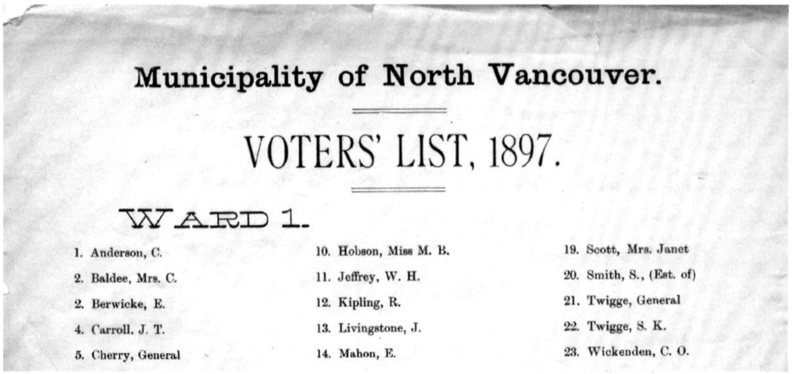

Municipality of North Vancouver.

VOTERS' LIST, 1897.

WARD 1.

1. Anderson, C.
2. Baldee, Mrs. C.
2. Berwicke, E.
4. Carroll, J. T.
5. Cherry, General

10. Hobson, Miss M. B.
11. Jeffrey, W. H.
12. Kipling, R.
13. Livingstone, J.
14. Mahon, E.

19. Scott, Mrs. Janet
20. Smith, S., (Est. of)
21. Twigge, General
22. Twigge, S. K.
23. Wickenden, C. O.

The District of North Vancouver was incorporated as an organized community in 1891. Property owners, most of whom had invested in land but did not actually live on the North Shore, had decided the previous winter that the time had come to form a municipality. They were encouraged by the creation of Vancouver in 1886 and the spurt of growth that the city subsequently experienced. Property values soared amid a frenzy of building and speculation. Why could not the same expansion occur on the north side of the inlet?

At the end of 1890 the proponents of incorporation held meetings in Vancouver to discuss their options. They agreed to petition the provincial government to create a municipality. Events moved quickly and the District of North Vancouver was inaugurated by letters patent dated August 10, 1891. The new district stretched from Horseshoe Bay in the west to Deep Cove in the east, excluding the First Nations reserves, which belonged to the federal government, and the two lots (DL 272 and 273) that comprised Moodyville. In total, the new district encompassed about 25,900 hectares (64,000 acres) extending from the waterfront up the flanks of the North Shore Mountains.

Top: During a visit to Vancouver in 1892, the writer Rudyard Kipling purchased a lot in North Vancouver, making him eligible to vote in the local election in 1897. By then he was back in England and did not cast a ballot.

Preceding pages: One of the earliest residents of Lynn Valley was George Smith, shown here outside his property on Campbell Avenue in 1909. Shaketown was still an isolated community, a long way from the business centres of Moodyville and Lower Lonsdale. NVMA 26-19D-8

Tom Turner's house, once a saloon, was the birthplace of North Vancouver where polling took place for the election of the District's first government in 1891. NVMA 251

On August 22, 1891, the district's handful of registered voters elected their first government, Reeve C. J. P. Phibbs and four councillors. Polling took place at Tom Turner's farmhouse, which was located at the foot of what is now Chesterfield Avenue. This humble cabin, formerly a saloon operated by Turner's uncle, William Bridge, can be called the birthplace of North Vancouver. High on the agenda for the new council was the need for roads to open the municipality to development. Thanks to local land promoter James Cooper Keith, who underwrote a loan on council's behalf, work commenced on a road that would eventually extend across the District from one end to the other.

Progress was slow. The North Shore was covered in thick forests and rock was very close to the surface. Heavy rainfall and the steep terrain led to constant flooding in some seasons. Roads, bridges, water lines and sewers all were vulnerable to washout and collapse. It was several years before Keith Road was finished—and even then it was rough going in places—but it was a start. Today Keith Road, sometimes under different names and not always contiguous, remains a major thoroughfare carrying traffic across the North Shore.

Every bit as important as the creation of a government was the formation that same year of the North Vancouver Land and Improvement Company. The NVLIC

Hotel North Vancouver overlooked the waterfront on the Esplanade west of Lonsdale. The grounds of the hotel, opened by Peter Larson in 1902, served as a public park and picnic area for visitors from around the inlet. NVMA 709

James Cooper Keith, prominent investor and land promoter, was the second reeve of the district. He guaranteed the loan that allowed the district to go ahead with the construction of Keith Road.
NVMA 106-15-2

was a group of British investors, led by a wealthy Anglo-Irish landowner named John Mahon, with high ambitions for the North Shore. John Mahon sent one of his younger brothers, Edward, out to British Columbia to manage and extend his investments, and it is Edward, through the NVLIC, who is closely associated with the growth of North Vancouver. The company obtained several lots in the new District and began making them available for purchase by settlers. The first "stump farmers" settled in the vicinity of what is now 15th Street and Lonsdale, commuting downhill along a rough logging road to the ferry wharf and across the inlet to Vancouver. The 1901 census revealed a District population of 365 people.

Two other prominent speculators also acquired property. Alfred St. George

The first District Hall, at Lonsdale Avenue and 1st Street, decked out to celebrate Dominion Day in 1906. When the City of North Vancouver separated from the District, this became city hall. NVMA 45

Alfred St. George Hamersley subdivided his property in Lower Lonsdale and began the residential development of the area. His palatial home, which still stands on 2nd Street, has received national historic designation. NVMA 4583

Hamersley, a well-to-do Vancouver lawyer, purchased the District lot to the south of the NVLIC lands straddling Lonsdale Avenue, called it the Town of Lonsdale and subdivided it into lots. And on either side of Hamersley's property, the Lonsdale Estate, another syndicate of British investors, owned significant holdings. With all these wealthy promoters vying to make money from their assets, the District experienced a period of impressive development, focused on the emerging commercial centre at the bottom of Lonsdale Avenue. One important landmark was the Hotel North Vancouver, opened on the Esplanade just west of Lonsdale by Peter Larson, a Swedish immigrant, in 1902. At that time the Esplanade was much closer to the waterfront than it is today. With lawns running down to the shore, the hotel became a favoured resort for people from Vancouver who came to enjoy the beach, the bandstand and the annual Canada Day celebrations. In 1903 the District could finally afford to build a municipal hall, at the corner of 1st Street and Lonsdale, where the council began meeting instead of in downtown Vancouver. The ferry service across Burrard Inlet was improved. The first school opened in 1902, along with the first bank in 1905. The District's first newspaper, the *Express*, began publishing in 1905. A system of pipes brought drinking water from Lynn Creek, and on Labour Day in 1906 the BC Electric Railway Company (BCER) opened a streetcar line up Lonsdale from the ferry wharf as far as 12th Street. This was just three weeks after the first electric lights lit the streets of the young community. In other words, the District was acquiring all the amenities of a modern municipality.

THE SMALLEST STREETCAR SYSTEM

Public transit arrived in North Vancouver on September 3, 1906, when the BC Electric Railway Company put a trio of tram cars into service on Lonsdale Avenue. It was the fourth, and smallest, operation in the BCER's streetcar network. Earlier street railway service had commenced in Victoria (February 1890), Vancouver (June 1890) and New Westminster (October 1891).

With the ferry connecting the North Shore to downtown Vancouver from the foot of Lonsdale, the streetcars naturally began at the ferry wharf. The first line ran up Lonsdale as far as 12th Street, later extending up the hill as far as Windsor Road. Before the year ended, it was joined by a second line running east to Grand Boulevard. And by 1911 a western line ran all the way to the Capilano River. *Continued on next page*

Three streetcars converge at the corner of First Street and Lonsdale Avenue, two blocks from the ferry wharf, ca. 1908. The white building facing First is the District Hall (later the City Hall). NVMA 3224

The streetcars provided convenient, efficient service for many years, but not without the occasional mishap. One August afternoon in 1909, the brakes failed on a car coming down Lonsdale to meet the 4 p.m. ferry. With fifteen passengers screaming in terror, the out-of-control car sped down the hill and off the end of the dock, into the harbour. The conductor leapt for safety, breaking his leg, while the passengers were fished safely from the water.

Accidents were few and far between, however, during the forty years the streetcars remained in service. They were eventually mothballed in 1947 when the BCER converted all its operations from trams to buses. Track and trolley wire were removed, streets repaved, and within a few months, all evidence of the old streetcars had gone.

The Lynn Valley streetcar on Lynn Valley Road in front of the District Hall, 1910. NVMA 8984

Three streetcars arrive at the foot of Lonsdale Avenue to meet the ferry in 1913. The area has become a busy commercial centre. NVMA 13442

HOW DID LONSDALE GET ITS NAME?

The original Lonsdale after whom North Vancouver's main street is named was Arthur Pemberton Heywood-Lonsdale, a wealthy British investor and speculator. Along with a relation, James P. Fell, Heywood-Lonsdale formed the Lonsdale Estate, a collection of properties around the Lower Mainland that included investments in the Moodyville sawmill as well as large portions of what became the city of North Vancouver. Heywood-Lonsdale died in 1897, just as his confidence in the future of the North Shore was bearing fruit.

Every inch the English country gentleman, Arthur Pemberton Heywood-Lonsdale, after whom Lonsdale Avenue is named, was a prominent investor in real estate and in the Moodyville sawmill company.
Courtesy Robert Heywood

Thomas Nye, shown with his wife, Emily, was a pioneer promoter of settlement in Upper Lonsdale.
NVMA 6705

It was also growing geographically. One of the first neighbourhoods to develop outside the central core was North (or Upper) Lonsdale, originally known as "Spar Hill" for the fine stands of tall timber logged to produce ships' masts. In 1902 a Boer War veteran named Thomas Nye received 160 acres (64.7 ha) of land in the vicinity of what is now Lonsdale Avenue and 29th Street in recognition of his military service. Nye joined just three other settlers who were living so far from the water, their remote lots connecting to "civilization" via a rough trail running down the hill through the trees. Nye built an impressive home for himself and sold some of his lots to other pioneers. The house, which still stands, is known today as "Nye's Folly" because he went broke trying to finish it. (His real estate office also survives, as a private residence.) Another promoter of the neighbourhood was Jack Loutet, whose real estate company handled many North Lonsdale properties. Loutet went on to have a long career in local government, serving as District councillor, District reeve, City mayor and member of the provincial legislature. (His son Lindsay, an enthusiastic skier, created the Grouse Mountain Ski Club in 1927. An excellent photographer, his mountain scenes document the early years on the North Shore ski hills.)

Within a few years Lonsdale Avenue extended north as far as Queens Road, the street railway had arrived, and North Lonsdale, with its spectacular views and a 1912 population of 180 families, was being hailed in the *North Shore Express* newspaper as "the premier residential district of Greater Vancouver."[11] The District created Carisbrooke Park, or "North Lonsdale Park" as it was known until the 1950s, as an elegant green space for residents of the upscale neighbourhood. There was even a lighted bandstand for local concerts. On weekends the park was a gathering spot for hikers and skiers who had taken the streetcar up Lonsdale and were organizing themselves for the long trek up the slopes of Grouse Mountain.

By this time, ratepayers in the District's commercial core, including the large land speculators, had decided to establish their own government. They thought it would be advantageous to create a smaller, more concentrated municipality with less responsibility for providing services to the large, but as yet sparsely populated, outlying area. Support for

Jean Waddell takes a snowy walk with her dog in Carisbrooke Park in 1917. For years the park, located at the end of the streetcar line, was a jumping-off spot for hikers heading into the mountains. NVMA 9837

Some of the leading promoters of the City of North Vancouver gather at City Hall to celebrate Dominion Day, July 1, 1907. City mayor Arnold Kealy is seated in the centre, flanked by J. C. Keith to his right and Edward Mahon to his left. NVMA 96

secession from the District built during 1905—there was really no one to speak for the interests of the fewer residents who lived beyond the central core—and culminated in a December referendum endorsing the creation of a new city, also called North Vancouver. ("Burrard" was the only other name given serious consideration but ratepayers decided to stick with the familiar.) Delays ensued but finally the details were resolved and the City of North Vancouver was incorporated on May 13, 1907. There were now two North Vancouvers: a City centred on the spine of Lonsdale Avenue surrounded on three sides by a much larger District. (The City gradually took over the land that had comprised Moodyville until, by 1925, all of it was absorbed.)

Gertrude Radcliff stands at the door of her tent home, ca. 1920. Her sister Sarah Cosgrove is seated beneath the umbrella. Modest homes like this one were a common sight in North Vancouver. NVMA 10721

TENT CITY

By 1911 the *Express* was calling North Vancouver "The City of Homes." Land was inexpensive and the community was conveniently close to downtown Vancouver, where commuters could work and shop. Real estate companies offered building lots for very little money down and easy payment terms. But many would-be homeowners of modest means, having purchased their property, could not afford to build their dream house, at least not yet. Instead they erected temporary housing in the form of tents and lived in them, sometimes for several years, while they accumulated a nest egg to begin construction. These "starter homes" were a common sight across the North Shore in the years before World War I.

Living in Shaketown

With the secession of the central core, the commercial and social centre of the District shifted to Lynn Valley, where logging had been going on since the 1870s. Initially the Moodyville company logged the Lynn Creek watershed mainly for Douglas fir. Loggers used axes to fell the giant trees, then removed the limbs and cut the trunks into manageable lengths. Oxen dragged the logs from the bush down skid roads to tidewater. These "roads" were necessary because the creeks on the North Shore are deep and narrow, not suited to the log drives more familiar on larger rivers. A skid road was constructed of logs laid crosswise to the slope, about 2.5 metres in width, with a U-shaped notch cut down the centre of the road. A greaser carrying a pail and brush went ahead of the oxen to slather the notch with dogfish oil to ensure a smooth run for the logs. The oil was produced from fish caught by the local First Nations, who sold it to the lumber companies.

Above left: Early Lynn Valley was known as Shaketown because so many of the buildings were made of cedar shakes. This hand-drawn map by Walter Draycott shows the tiny logging community, the tote road and the flume that carried shingle bolts down to Moodyville. NVMA Fonds 26, Inventory 18, Box 26

The corner of Lynn Valley Road and Fromme Road in 1910 before much settlement had occurred in the area. Shaketown, the centre of the community, is located a few blocks farther north. NVMA 26-19H-12

Shingles, or shakes, were thin pieces of cedar cut from a larger block, or bolt, of wood. These men (right and opposite) are illustrating the process of sawing, rolling and bundling shingles at the Horne Brothers mill.
Right: NVMA 1120-18; opposite: NVMA 1120-10

Below: Teams hauling shingle bolts down a plank road near Rice Lake. NVMA 9087

Above: The abundance of western red cedar on the North Shore Mountains led to a boom in the shingle industry. Once sawn, the shingles passed to the bundler (shown here), where they were bundled for shipment. NVMA 1988.77.1 Shawn McDonald photo

Below: A detail from a 1912 map showing the route of the Lynn Valley flume down to tidewater. NVMA 26-26-1

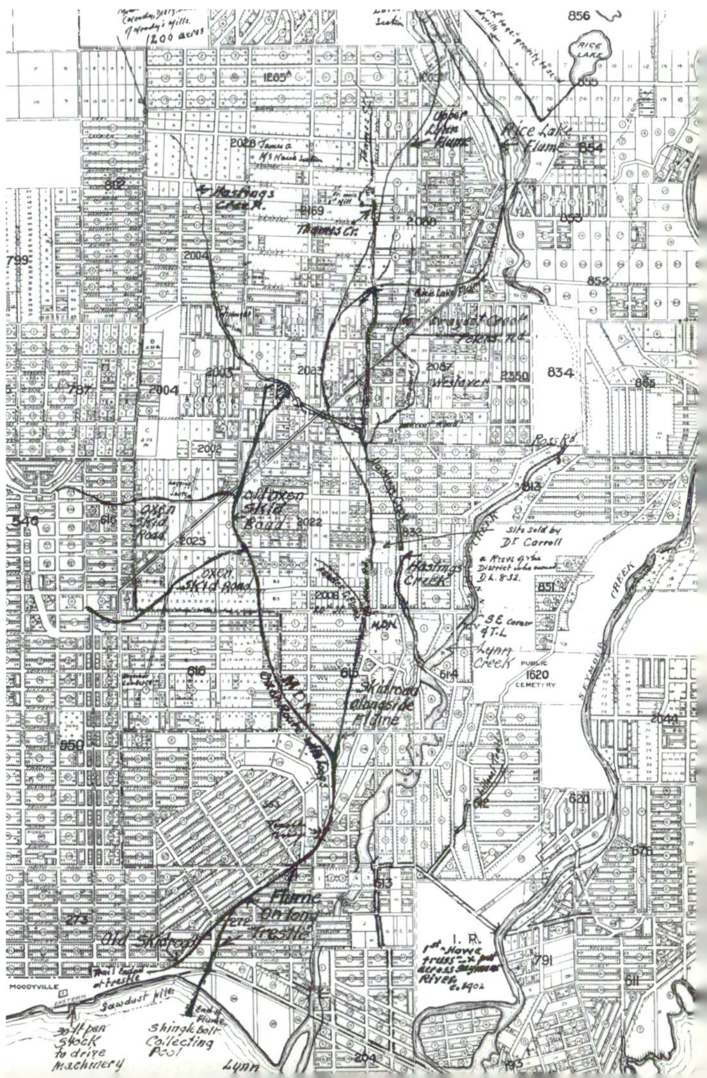

Japanese logging camp at Rice Lake, 1905. A group of Japanese families operated a mill at Rice Lake for many years. Japanese work crews also helped to build shingle bolt flumes. NVMA 26-19E-7

After about 1890 the production of cedar shingles became a booming industry around Burrard Inlet. Wood shingles had not yet been surpassed by asphalt as the main roofing material in North America and red cedar made the best product. Shingles were made from lengths of cedar that were split into wedge-shaped blocks known as "shingle bolts" and either floated down a flume to the mill or hauled down the skid road. The number of shingle mills in BC rose dramatically, from 9 in 1891 to 93 by the middle of World War I. BC mills, most of them located in the Lower Mainland, produced the vast majority of the shingles manufactured in Canada, and exported them throughout the United States.

In 1895 H. H. Spicer leased timber rights in the Lynn Creek area from the Moodyville company and began cutting shingle bolts. Spicer's men built several kilometres of flumes to carry the bolts to a collection pond near the present Park and Tilford shopping centre. The flume was a marvel of construction, consisting of a broad wooden trough elevated above the forest floor on a wooden trestle. When filled with water from the creek or a lake, it carried the bolts down the flume to tidewater. (Prospectors were also active in Lynn Creek, scouring the watershed

James McNair, "the shingle king of the Northwest," built one of the fanciest homes in North Vancouver with the fortune he made from his shingle mills. NVMA 9179

for signs of gold or zinc and staking their claims. But the area, which was remote and rugged, lacked good roads and was never the site of any significant mineral discovery.)

After two years Spicer sold his operation to the Hastings Shingle Manufacturing Company, a Vancouver-based company owned by the McNair brothers, James and Robert. The McNairs, who originally came from New Brunswick, had established their first mill in the Hastings Townsite at the south end of the Second Narrows. They had done so well specializing in the manufacture of cedar shingles that the elder brother, James, was known as "the shingle

A group of loggers pose with their equipment near Fromme's mill in Lynn Valley, 1909. NVMA 464

246. Hauling Logs
Lynn Valley Lbr Co
No. Vancouver B.C.

Bucksaws were used by loggers in the woods before the introduction of power saws. This one dates to about 1890. NVMA 2000.20.23
Shawn McDonald photo

Above: A logging crew, including three Chinese men, hauls a length of cedar down the skid road to the mill in Lynn Valley in the days of horse logging. NVMA 3869

Opposite top left: A logging crew poses with the tools of their trade, simple axes and a crosscut saw. NVMA 10014

Opposite top right: Hauling logs down a Lynn Valley skid road using a team of horses. NVMA 26-19E-3

Left: Towering cedar trees like this one, with a stump 3.6 metres across, attracted early loggers to the forested slopes of the North Shore Mountains. NVMA 1247

king of the northwest." James McNair built a house in North Vancouver City on East 6th Street at a cost of fifteen thousand dollars, a fortune at the time. Still standing today, it was considered one of the most palatial homes in the Lower Mainland, with a wraparound verandah, ornate fireplaces and beautiful hardwood finishings imported from as far away as Australia.

The McNairs extended logging operations northward, up Lynn Canyon and into the Rice Lake area where they

Above: Julius Fromme owned the Lynn Valley Lumber Company and promoted the early development of "Shaketown." His home still stands on Ross Road. NVMA 6625

Left: Goodwin Johnson poses between a pair of giant firs, 1918. NVMA 1139

Above: A Lynn Valley Lumber Company crew pose on a shingle bolt sled in 1906. Julius Fromme is standing on the right in a white shirt. The company logged off much of the Lynn Creek watershed. NVMA 104

Left: Four loggers, with dog, pose at the foot of a giant fir in Lynn Valley. NVMA 63

had a shingle bolt camp. As they moved farther up the slope, they decided to build a mill to provide the lumber necessary for their network of flumes and plank roads, much of which was constructed by Chinese labour. Opened in 1903, this operation came to be called the "Upper Mill" and was managed by Julius Fromme. It was located in upper Lynn Valley above what is now Dempsey Road. In 1906, when the McNairs decided to close the business, Fromme and a partner purchased the mill and established the Lynn Valley Lumber Company. Fromme was "the first resident and real founder of Lynn Valley,"[12] in the words of historian Kathleen Woodward-Reynolds. He had purchased land near the present day corner of Lynn Valley Road and Mountain Highway, which he subdivided and sold to mill workers, and pretty soon a small settlement of bunkhouses and cabins emerged, known as "Shaketown." Fromme opened a second mill nearby, the so-called "Lower Mill." It produced mainly shakes from bolts that came down Hastings Creek to a collecting pond. Both mills continued in business into the 1920s.

Downtown Lynn Valley, the corner of Mountain Highway and Lynn Valley Road, in 1914. The Sanitary Grocery occupies part of what was called the "Triangle Block." The Fromme Block across the street was home to J. Barker Hardware for many years. NVMA 2929

CLASSROOM PIONEER

Mollie Nye belonged to a pioneering Lynn Valley family. Her father, Jack Nye, like his brother Thomas, was a veteran of the Boer War and received a grant of 160 acres of land on what later became Lynn Valley Road. Mollie, who was born in 1913, grew up at the family home and lived there most of her life. Following in the footsteps of her mother, Mollie became a schoolteacher, most notably at Sutherland School where she was on faculty for twenty-two years. Outside the classroom she was a community activist involved in all manner of clubs and organizations. Mollie retired from Sutherland in 1972, and in her retirement, kept up an active round of activities in Lynn Valley. When she died in 1997 she left her family's home to the District of North Vancouver and it stands today as Mollie Nye House, a community services centre.

Mollie Nye (r.) with her sister Joyce in 1925. Both girls became schoolteachers, Mollie most prominently in North Vancouver. NVMA 7837

For a brief period from 1917 to 1926, Fromme faced competition from another logging outfit, Cedars Ltd., owned by M. P. Cotton and his associates. Taking advantage of the strong demand for cedar, this company built a mill on the east bank of Lynn Creek about 5 kilometres above Fromme's mill. It built a network of plank roads and was notable for employing motorized trucks to haul the timber, the first company on the North Shore to go in for truck logging. By the mid-1920s officials in the City and the District were worried about the impact of logging on the quality of drinking water from the watershed. After much debate, in 1928 the Lynn Creek watershed was closed to commercial logging, by which time the timber supply had petered out anyway.

Earlier, Robert McNair had created a second company, the McNair-Fraser Lumber Company, with the sole purpose of harvesting wood for the Vancouver mill run by his brother James. McNair-Fraser concentrated its operations west of the Capilano River, in what later became West Vancouver. In 1907 McNair-Fraser established a log dump at Ambleside and began to construct a logging railway up the slope into what became the British Properties and beyond. Eventually McNair-Fraser sold its timber rights, but logging continued in this area into the 1920s.

A major mill operation also was located on the eastern border between the City and District. For years the Western Corporation, a development company with headquarters in the Syndicate Block at Lonsdale and Esplanade, had been importing lumber and building supplies from Vancouver by tug and scow and delivering them to building sites across the North Shore by horse and wagon. In 1906 the company decided to open its own sawmill, a large complex between 16th and 18th Streets, just east of Grand Boulevard. This mill, which employed about eighty men, produced much of the lumber used for building in the early days of the District and City, using logs that it skidded down from the slopes of Grouse Mountain. The newly constructed street railway provided flat cars on which the lumber travelled from the mill yard to the waterfront. When the Western Corporation went bankrupt in 1909, the mill continued in operation as the Seymour Lumber Company until May 1912, when it was destroyed by fire.

As this photograph illustrates, the Seymour Lumber Company employed a multi-ethnic labour force, including Chinese, First Nations, Sikh and Japanese workers.
NVMA 257

LYNN VALLEY PIONEER

Walter Draycott was one of Lynn Valley's pioneer settlers. He purchased several lots in 1912, when he was twenty-nine years old, and built a home on what became Draycott Road. He recorded his initial impressions of the area: "There were the snow-capped and forested slopes of mountains, the rivers in which hundreds of salmon cavorted, trees of astounding height and girth, waterfalls and the pools below were alive with leaping salmon, deep rock canyons that beckoned the venturesome . . . bears, deer, cougar, racoon and the delightful squirrel, and the 'baldheaded' eagle and smaller birds . . . Where on this globe would one find such a desirable setting to live and enjoy the freedom it offered?"[13]

When World War I began, Walter Draycott volunteered for the Canadian army and, during four years overseas, saw action on the Western Front, twice surviving gas attacks. He returned to Lynn Valley in 1918 and lived the rest of his life there, serving in many community groups and organizations. For fifty years he was a Justice of the Peace and was an informal historical resource for the community. A lifelong bachelor, he lived modestly in his small house, indulging his wide interests in geology, photography, history and the natural sciences. His book, *Early Days in Lynn Valley*, appeared in 1978.

Walter Draycott kept a daily diary for his entire adult life, almost eighty years. Since his death in 1985 at the age of 102, these journals have become an invaluable source of information about life on the North Shore.

Walter Draycott at his home on Draycott Road, 1920s. NVMA 26-6-24

The District Hall on Lynn Valley Road not long after it opened in 1911. A low stone wall later separated the hall property from the sidewalk; today it is all that remains of the original structure. NVMA 11861

Because the municipal hall remained in the City when it separated, the District had no office of its own for several years. The first meeting of District council occurred on June 10, 1907, in the Lynn Valley School, which had opened three years earlier, and the first elections were held in tents and private homes. It wasn't until August 1911 that the district hall opened at the intersection of Lynn Valley Road and Fromme Road. (It remained at this location until it was replaced by a new hall at its present, more central location on Queens Road in the 1950s.) For many years Shaketown's only connection to the outside world was a plank road running down to Moodyville along the route that is today Mountain Highway. As the community grew, so did the desire for improvements to the transportation network. By early 1907

During a heavy snowfall in January 1913, District engineering staff take advantage of the lunch hour to toss snowballs on Lynn Valley Road. NVMA 113

the streetcar line ascended Grand Boulevard as far as 19th Street, with a plank road extending north from there to Shaketown. Electricity and telephone service followed and then, in May 1910, the street railway itself trundled up what is now Lynn Valley Road to a terminus at Dempsey Road, making this once-isolated neighbourhood more easily accessible to the City and beyond.

By this time, residents had formed the Lynn Valley Institute, a social club and community centre based at a hall on Institute Road. Institute activities included choir singing, amateur theatrics, debates and, in 1911, the first music festival in the province. Postal service was provided by Mrs. Alice Sugden, who drove to Lower Lonsdale every day in a horse-drawn carriage to pick up the mail and bring it back to the post office, which was in her home. In 1912, when the Fromme Block opened at the corner of Lynn Valley Road and Centre Road, later Mountain Highway, the post office moved into it and the street railway brought the mail. All of these improvements made the Lynn Valley area a more desirable place to settle and, by 1919, the community had a population of about 1,400. "It was a period in which there were virtually no restrictions," recalled Walter Draycott, with more than a hint of nostalgia. "You fished without a licence and none was needed to hunt, light a fire or pan for gold. In fact, no 'Don'ts.' According to your desire you built a cabin, erected a tent or lean-to anywhere along the river or in the woods. You hiked where you pleased . . . Truly, the 'Good Old Days!'"[14]

Postmistress Alice Sugden in her carriage, 1909.
NVMA 26-27-39

BOHEMIAN IN THE VALLEY

Frederick Varley, a founding member of the famous Group of Seven painters from Toronto and the best portraitist among them, arrived in Vancouver in 1926 to teach painting at the newly established Vancouver School of Decorative and Applied Arts (VSA), now the Emily Carr University of Art + Design. Perhaps the most bohemian of the Group members in his lifestyle, Varley was invigorated by the West Coast landscape and his stay in Vancouver produced some of the best work of his career. When the Depression arrived and the VSA slashed his salary, Varley established his own school, the BC College of Arts, with fellow painter Jock Macdonald. Though short-lived, art historian Dennis Reid has called the school "the centre of Vancouver's cultural life" at the time.[15]

Varley was very popular with his students, whom he used to take hiking in the North Shore Mountains. On one of these excursions in 1934, he came across an empty cabin overlooking Lynn Creek at the top of Lynn Valley Road. He found out it was vacant and rented it for eight dollars a week. Varley lived there with his young mistress, Vera Weatherbie, while his wife, Maud, and the children lived in Vancouver. He was extremely poor during this period, and drinking heavily, but he later recalled it as one of the happiest periods of his life. In 1936 he left BC and returned to Ontario. Maud then moved into the cabin with their children; eventually she bought the place and lived there for several years.

Today there is a short hiking trail named for Varley in Lynn Headwaters Regional Park.

A Canyon Playground

Once West Vancouver formed its own municipality in 1912, the Capilano River became the western edge of the District of North Vancouver. The Squamish village of Homulcheson was located at its mouth, but the valley of the Capilano was not yet extensively settled by outsiders. Still, it was known and valued for two resources: water and wood. When the new City of Vancouver was created on the south shore of Burrard Inlet, its municipal leaders sought a source of clean drinking water for the population they knew would be growing rapidly. They found what they were looking for in the Capilano where, as Chief Engineer H. B. Smith reported,

The original Vancouver Waterworks Company dam where the pipeline carrying water to Vancouver originated. The site is now beneath Capilano Lake. NVMA 87

"No purer water can be obtained from any source than that from this mountain stream."[16] The job of delivering water from the river to Vancouver was given to a private syndicate, the Vancouver Waterworks Company. It built a dam high up the valley, snaked a pipeline alongside the river for 10.5 kilometres down to tidewater, and laid a water main beneath the First Narrows and across Stanley Park into the city. It was an unprecedented engineering achievement for its time. On March 26, 1889, water from the Capilano began flowing into Vancouver homes and businesses. (Today the river continues to deliver about one-third of the water

Above: The Capilano Suspension Bridge during the World War I era, supported by steel cables but still a daunting prospect for anyone fearful of heights. The sign warns visitors: DO NOT SHAKE THE BRIDGE. NVMA 52

Left: In 1905, when this photograph was taken, a trip to the suspension bridge was a real undertaking. Visitors arrived by horse and wagon and it would have taken much of a day to get there. NVMA 330

Above: Charlie Anderson displays his catch at the salmon pool in the Capilano River. Anderson was the proprietor of the Tipperary Tea Garden at the Second Canyon, opened during World War I. NVMA 5213

Right: The poet Pauline Johnson (l.) visits the Capilano Hotel with her friend Lizzie Timms, wife of the Vancouver photographer Philip Timms, who took this shot. NVMA 8255

The Canyon View Hotel at the time of its opening. It was located where the Cleveland Dam is today. NVMA 100

consumed in Metro Vancouver. All water consumed in the District and City of North Vancouver originates in either the Capilano or Seymour watersheds. Since the spring of 2010 this water has been filtered at the Seymour-Capilano Filtration Plant located near Rice Lake in the Lower Seymour Conservation Reserve.)

The water company—which became a public utility in 1891—built a wagon road to service its pipeline and this became Capilano Road. For several years it was the only way to access the Capilano area. There was a wharf at the foot of the road, where visitors would disembark and hike up the road to fish in the river or climb in the mountains. After the turn of the century, people could also take the ferry to North Vancouver, then make their way westward along Keith Road to the river. In 1906 Dickson Kells, a Vancouver hotelier, opened the Capilano Hotel near the water dam at a site that is now beneath Capilano Lake. He offered rooms to hikers, anglers, climbers and hunters, all of whom were attracted by the recreational possibilities of the valley. He also provided a "tally-ho" service, a horse and wagon to pick up and drop off customers at the Lonsdale ferry. Access to the area was much improved in

Two colour postcards show the Capilano flume winding its way through the canyon. It was the impassable nature of the canyon that necessitated the construction of a flume to carry shingle bolts to tidewater. Top: NVMA 8862; bottom: NVMA 3291

who used to "walk the flume" (actually the catwalk) to penetrate the steep walls of the canyon. It was demolished as a safety hazard sometime in the late 1920s.

Eventually American logging interests became interested in the valley of the Capilano. In 1908 a syndicate based in Chicago created the Capilano Timber Company to exploit the forest resources of the area. The market was not strong enough to allow the company to proceed with its plans until World War I, when conditions improved. By 1919 the Capilano Timber Company had pushed a logging railway 25.5 kilometres back into the watershed from its mill near the

Above: Climax locomotive used on the Capilano Timber Company's logging railway. NVMA 1072

Left: The Capilano Timber Company mill on the water at the foot of Pemberton Avenue during the height of its operations in the mid-1920s. Fire destroyed the mill in 1932. NVMA 1328

foot of Pemberton Avenue. (The site is now occupied by Vancouver Shipyards, owned by Seaspan.) The track ran north to Marine Drive, then west below Pemberton Heights to the Capilano, which it crossed on a wooden trestle into West Vancouver. It then proceeded north up the west side of the river. The company ran a state-of-the-art camp beyond the upper end of Capilano Lake, where logs were collected and loaded onto the railway for transport down to the inlet. At its height during the mid-1920s the operation employed 175 men. Logging had a devastating impact on the environment. A large swath of the Capilano Valley was denuded of trees

This colour postcard shows the Cleveland Dam, the Capilano Lake reservoir behind it and, in the distance, the twin peaks of the Lions. NVMA 6706

and covered in slash. Fires became more prevalent and officials feared the possibility of a widespread conflagration. With the undergrowth destroyed, water runoff became heavier, leading to soil erosion and regular flooding in the river. The worst flooding occurred in 1949 when rushing water carried away part of the bridge at Marine Drive and West Vancouver was cut off from North Vancouver. Following this mishap, flood control measures in the river had the unintended consequence of wiping out valuable salmon spawning grounds. Between these measures and the opening of the Cleveland Dam in 1954, salmon stocks in the river fell sharply until the opening of the Capilano Salmon Hatchery in 1971 reversed the decline.

In the end, the river proved more valuable as a source of clean water than a source of timber. In 1926 the province created the Greater Vancouver Water District to manage and protect the local watersheds. The GVWD, led by Chief Commissioner E. A. Cleveland, pressured the logging company to abandon its

Ernest Cleveland was an American-born civil engineer practising in Vancouver when he was appointed first Chief Commissioner of the Greater Vancouver Water District in 1926. The creation of the district eventually closed the Capilano watershed to logging. NVMA 757

operations in the Capilano Valley. In 1932 a spectacular fire destroyed the company's waterfront mill, and by the end of the following year, commercial logging had ceased in the watershed. Even so, the damage was long-lasting. As recently as the 1990s, homeowners were experiencing turbidity (cloudy drinking water) as a result of soil erosion on denuded slopes. Some regulated logging continued in the Capilano and Seymour watersheds into the 1990s to clear diseased trees, protect against fire and otherwise manage the health of the forest. In the face of public protest, even this limited logging came to an end.

Just as it had in North Lonsdale and Lynn Valley, the arrival of the streetcar in the Lower Capilano facilitated business opportunities and residential developments.

Students at Capilano School in 1914–1915. Many of their fathers would have been loggers working in the woods. The school was located on the present site of the Capilano Tennis Club. NVMA 4327

The first school opened in 1906, the so-called "little green schoolhouse," catering to loggers' families and those of the odd settler. Once the logging railway was in operation, men could leave their homes in Lower Capilano and ride the train into the valley to work in the bush. By the 1920s the population of the neighbourhood numbered about two hundred. One focal point of the community was a general store and post office located at the end of the streetcar line, established by Norman MacLeod in 1911. MacLeod had the only telephone in the area; he charged four cents to make a call. He also owned a motorcar, in which he drove visitors who got off the streetcar up to the suspension bridge for fifteen cents. A medical clinic operated out of the back of the store. (The store and the area around the streetcar terminus were destroyed by the construction of the Upper Levels Highway in 1960.)

Marine Drive was still a rural area in the 1920s, with several dairy farms in business on either side of the road. One unusual destination was the home of Napoleon St. Pierre at the corner of MacGowan Avenue. St. Pierre filled his garden with sculpted shrubs and offered to tell fortunes and read horoscopes for a fee. On Sundays the car traffic outside his house was so heavy as to block the road. Across the street, a

Harbottle's Jersey Products, founded by Thomas Harbottle, offered North Vancouver's first home milk delivery. In 1938 Harbottle purchased this one-ton Diamond T pickup to use as a delivery vehicle. He sold his business in 1942 and the truck ended up in a scrapyard where it was rescued, restored and donated to the North Vancouver Museum by Harbottle's son Jeffery. NVMA Fonds 44 series 5 dairy farmer named Billy Wilkins (known as the "yodelling milkman") opened his own establishment, the Dew Drop Inn, where along with a cup of tea, patrons were treated to the predictions of an Indian fortune teller, complete with turban.

Chief Mathias Joe Capilano with the profusion of First Nations artifacts inside the Tomahawk Restaurant. NVMA 10629

THE TOMAHAWK RESTAURANT

The Tomahawk is said to be the oldest family-run eatery in Canada. In the 1920s Chick Chamberlain and his brother opened a coffee shop in their cabins-to-rent operation on Marine Drive at Heywood Park. In 1926 Chick moved west down Marine Drive to what is now Norgate, and opened his own restaurant, the original Tomahawk Barbecue, a dozen or so stools inside and the Vancouver area's first drive-in outside. Now located on Philip Avenue, the restaurant has been a popular neighbourhood hangout from the beginning. Today it is known for its collection of First Nations artifacts, many of them carved by members of the Squamish Nation who live nearby, as well as huge servings of burgers and pancakes. Rock star Bryan Adams once worked as a dishwasher at the Tomahawk.

Depression and Recovery

During the economic depression of the 1930s, times were as tough in North Vancouver as they were elsewhere in Canada and around the world. "Money had taken a long vacation," remarked Walter Draycott. Jobs dried up and residents scrambled to make a living any way they could. Homesteaders who tried to sell their properties discovered there were no buyers for their land. Instead they cut shingle bolts for the local mills and turned to foraging for food. "To augment the food supply," recalled Draycott, "occasional journeys were made down the old Tote or Skid-road to the mud flats at Moodyville to obtain clams. The journey back, all up-hill for nearly three miles, with a sack half-full of clams was a test of endurance. Hazelnuts were gathered along the estuary banks of Seymour Creek and trout, in plenty, along the canyon route of Lynn Creek. No fishing permit necessary!"[18]

Charles Tisdall, who served as first commissioner of the City and the District, had a long career in public administration. He was the mayor of Vancouver 1922–1923, as well as a provincial cabinet minister. NVMA 7874

Many property owners, unable to pay their taxes, lost their homes. With its tax revenues dwindling, the District government laid off workers because it could not pay them. Money that was previously borrowed for local improvements had to be repaid, but there was inadequate revenue to make the payments. Financial relief for the unemployed was yet another drain on the budget. Crucial to the financial ills of both the City and District was the closure of the Second Narrows Bridge, damaged when a freighter rammed it in mid-September 1930. The bridge, which remained closed for four years, had been financed by the sale of bonds. Both North Shore communities were shareholders in the bridge company, which was legally required to pay interest to bondholders. These payments were an onerous burden for local governments already suffering from the strains of the Depression.

Finally, in December 1932, the provincial government stepped in and appointed a commissioner to administer the affairs of the District: Charles Tisdall, a former sporting goods merchant, provincial cabinet minister and one-term mayor of Vancouver. The following month, Tisdall became commissioner of the City as well.

This scene shows a classroom in the Crosby School for Girls on Grand Boulevard in 1936. The school was founded in Victoria in 1921, then moved to North Vancouver in 1925. It closed in the 1940s. NVMA 5226

(Burnaby also went into commissionership at about the same time. West Vancouver avoided bankruptcy largely because, in 1931, British investors purchased from the municipality 1,620 hectares of land that became the British Properties development and gave jobs to many local men making improvements to the property.) The two elected North Vancouver councils were abolished. Tisdall took immediate steps to slash public services to a minimum, which meant layoffs and cutbacks. The municipalities had been contributing to the cost of unemployment relief, along with the province and the federal government, but by the middle of 1933, Tisdall reported that North Vancouver could no longer afford to pay its share. During that year only 38 percent of the assessed property tax revenues were actually collected; the following year that figure fell even lower, to 33.7 percent. Other austerity measures included the closure of the District hall and the centralizing of public administration in the City, along with the transference of policing from the local force to the BC Provincial Police. Tisdall and his successors ruled with the authority of dictators and managed to cut expenditures to the bone. Commissioner J. V. Fisher, who took over from Tisdall in 1934, reported that expenditures on municipal services had been slashed to 68 percent of what they had been prior to the Depression. Elected local government finally returned to the City in 1944, by which time the booming shipyards had brought renewed prosperity. The District, on the other hand, did not return to self-government until 1951.

One of the bright spots during the Depression was the success of the North Shore United soccer club, which won a national championship in 1938, led by star player Jimmy Spencer (r.). NVMA 13874

> "This condition had arisen from a variety of reasons, amongst them being unsound and inflated assessed values of real estate, continued borrowing and spending money, in many cases for services which were beyond the means of the taxpayer to pay for; covering too large an area with municipal services, the breaking down of a bridge [the Second Narrows] connecting the North Shore with Vancouver City, the world economic condition and resultant absence of work, financing of unemployment, unbalanced budgets and tax delinquency."
> —Charles Tisdall, commissioner of North Vancouver[19]

RELIEF WORKERS BUILT THE BLAIR RIFLE RANGE

During the Depression, the District was the site of one of the unemployed relief camps established by the federal government in response to the soaring numbers of men who could not find jobs in the shattered economy. In 1933 the Department of National Defence (DND) was given responsibility for managing these camps, seventy-three of which were located in British Columbia. Camp residents received accommodations, meals, health care and a daily stipend of twenty cents. The men worked mainly on road and airfield construction, but the North Vancouver camp, which opened on January 4, 1934, was on the site of the Blair Rifle Range in the Northlands area of the District.

Northlands was a 644-acre parcel of land, west of today's Parkgate shopping centre, expropriated from the District in 1927 by the DND. Three years later the Blair Rifle Range, named after Major R. M. Blair of the Seaforth Highlanders, opened on the site and the job of the relief camp workers, when they arrived, was to expand the facilities. The North Vancouver camp remained open for two and a half years, until the middle of 1936, during which time the men built roads, firing berms and several buildings.

Relief camps were unpopular with many of their occupants, who resented the military discipline that prevailed. Residents were free to leave, but if they did, they lost access to welfare. And where would they go when jobs were so scarce? In April 1935 hundreds of men left camps across BC and descended on Vancouver, where they staged a series of defiant demonstrations and eventually, early in June, boarded CPR freight trains in what has become known as the "On-to-Ottawa Trek." Some of these protestors came from the North Vancouver camp.

With the easing of the Depression, the federal government closed the relief camps at the end of June 1936, including the one at the Blair Rifle Range. During World War II, many different military units used the range for firearms, machine gun and grenade training. This continued after the war, when the RCMP also used the facility for firearms practice. By 1968 the DND had no more use for the range, but instead of selling it back to the District, it was sold to Central Mortgage and Housing, the federal government housing agency. Since that time, the property has been mired in a series of disputes between levels of government, and while residential development has occurred all around it, the old range remains empty.

Seymour and Deep Cove

At the eastern end of the District beyond the Seymour River, residential development was delayed for many years by lack of reliable access. The original Keith Road was supposed to cross the entire District but it was little more than a rough track into the 1930s, and the bridge across the Seymour was regularly damaged by flooding. The Dollarton Highway, which opened in 1931, provided an alternate connection, but the Second Narrows Bridge was so unreliable that travel from Vancouver was hit-and-miss. Northlands had a few pioneer residents by the 1930s, and there was a dairy farm at Maplewood, but not much else. Deep Cove itself (known originally as "Deepwater") was the site of a granite quarry until 1924. The quarry employed about one hundred men, who lived in bunkhouses on site and produced crushed rock for road work and other construction projects.

The other local industry was logging on the flanks of Mount Seymour. In 1917

Swimming at the dock in Deep Cove, ca. 1930. During its early history the Cove was a popular summer cottage community. NVMA 7944

the Deep Cove Lumber Company (DCLC), owned by Fred Buck, ran a 5-kilometre-long plank road up the mountain and began hauling out logs using 5-ton Duplex trucks. It was only the second truck-logging operation on the North Shore. Logs were brought to the shore at the bottom of what is now Gallant Avenue, the Cove's main street, dumped into the water, boomed and towed to nearby mills. The DCLC operated until 1926, when its supply of timber ran out. Aside from logging and the quarry, the Cove was mainly a summer cottage community with only a handful of permanent residents. During the thirties the George family converted the old quarry into a hotel, Quarries Lodge, and Corfield's Dance Hall on the waterfront attracted people from around the North Shore and even Vancouver to its lively Saturday night dances.

Today Deep Cove is a unique waterfront residential community. Alexandra Greenberg photo

Booming logs in Deep Cove, ca. 1912. NVMA 13968

> "The last few miles of the road run through virgin forest. It was really a one-way road with passing places about every half-mile; you had to keep your wheels on mill-planed boards to keep from bogging down in the rain-soaked earth, and be prepared to drive backwards if you met another vehicle."
> —Poet Earle Birney on driving Keith Road to Deep Cove in the 1920s[20]

Despite its remoteness, Indian Arm—or the "North Arm," as it was known officially until 1921—attracted sightseers and summer excursionists from as early as the 1880s, and even a handful of settlers who began to complain about the lack of access to their properties. By 1908 a regular ferry service from Vancouver delivered passengers to several points of call around the Arm, and a travelling post office brought the mail. (For many years, until it discontinued service in 1970, it was the only floating post office in the Commonwealth.) The only industry on the Arm, aside from a scattering of logging camps, was a granite quarry that operated for many years at Granite Falls, on the northeastern shore. In 1910 a group of Vancouver investors, spearheaded by B. F. "Benny" Dickens, built an elegant lodge, Wigwam Inn, at the head of the inlet, near the mouth of the Indian River. One of the other owners was the mysterious Alvo von Alvensleben, son of a German nobleman, who channelled millions of dollars from Europe into Vancouver business interests in the years before World War I. With the outbreak of war and the collapse of the local financial boom, he skipped town to avoid internment as an enemy alien. The Wigwam Inn changed hands several times over the years, and today belongs to the Royal Vancouver Yacht Club for use as

Top: Boating at Sunshine, a tiny cottage community on the western shore of Indian Arm, 1914. NVMA 10168

Bottom: This colour postcard shows Wigwam Inn during the 1920s. In its heyday as a hotel it had thirty-two bedrooms and a dining hall that seated one hundred. NVMA 5503

Wigwam Inn as it looks today as an outstation owned by the Royal Vancouver Yacht Club. NVMA 13366

Top: The floating grocery *Seabiscuit* making its rounds in Indian Arm, ca. 1950. Deep Cove Heritage Society 0432

Bottom: A group of excursionists travel up Indian Arm in 1913. NVMA 8722 an outstation. Much of the shoreline of Indian Arm was collected into Say Nuth Khaw Yum Provincial Park (also known as "Indian Arm Provincial Park") in 1995. Other mini-communities along the west side of the Arm include Woodlands (now with road access to the rest of the District), Sunshine, Cascade and Brighton Beach.

> "Marjorie Winfield is a pocket edition gal who is not only skipper, but first mate, engineer, navigator and crew of a 30-foot craft best known along Burrard Inlet as 'The Store Boat.' For almost six years now, spring, summer, fall and winter, good days and bad days and cold days, calm days and stormy ones, this small friendly woman has carried supplies to the scores of North Arm residents in her 'sailing supermarket.' When the boat pulls into any one of the dozen docks along the Arm, women clamber aboard with shopping bags to buy from the well-stocked shelves, to visit and to chat. The boat and its personable skipper carry not only the supplies but the news of the Inlet."
> —*Vancouver Province*, April 25, 1953

The lack of reliable road connections frustrated large-scale industrial development at the eastern end of the District. One exception was forestry at Roche Point, where Burrard Inlet rounds into Indian Arm. Known as "Whey-ah-Wichen" ("Facing the Wind") to the Tsleil-Waututh people, it has been occupied for at least 3,500 years. Prior to contact with Europeans, the Tsleil-Waututh's largest winter settlement was Temtemixwtn at Belcarra, but Whey-ah-Wichen was another important site where the Tsleil-Waututh lived in their large, multi-family,

Top: The Robert Dollar mill in 1918, shortly after it opened. It produced lumber for markets around the world until it closed during World War II. Modern homes now occupy the site of the mill. NVMA 3310

Bottom: A wood wagon and lumber tractor used at the Dollar Mill. NVMA 3311

Above: Senior staff members at the mill lived in houses like these in Dollarton. VPL 6535

Right: Robert Stirrat poses outside his general store on the Dollar Road with his children, Robert and Marion, in 1940. Following the war he opened a new store on the Dollarton Highway; it remained in business until 1968. NVMA 3337

Opposite right: Blacksmiths at work in the machine shop at the Dollar Mill, 1918. VPL 20572

Below: The entire workforce poses outside the Canadian Dollar Mill in 1937. Deep Cove Heritage Society 0629

1337.
DOMINION
PHOTO CO.
VANCOUVER, B.C.

STAFF OF CANADIAN ROBERT DOLLAR Co. LTD.
DOLLARTON, B.C. 1937

shed-roofed houses. The people fished for salmon and cod in the inlet, harvested clams and mussels along the shore, gathered herring spawn, and hunted deer, elk, bear, beaver and mountain goats. They also relied on a wide variety of plants for foods, medicines and implements, most notably the cedar dugout canoes in which they plied the waters of the inlet. Logging began at Roche Point in 1885 and, prior to World War I, a syndicate of investors made ambitious plans for an industrial centre there, including mills, shipbuilding, even a steelworks. Promoters, encouraged by plans for a Second Narrows Bridge and a rail line, spoke of the Point becoming the "Pittsburgh of the Northwest." The prewar recession scuttled these optimistic dreams. The only project that actually came to fruition was a sawmill opened by the Red Fir Lumber Company in 1910. Later called "Cedarside," it provided sawn cedar to a parent mill in False Creek. During World War I, the Canadian Robert Dollar Company purchased land to the north of Cedarside and, in 1917, established a much larger Dollar Mill. This mill shipped lumber all over the world. Workers lived with their families in the townsite that grew up nearby. "Each house has a garden," Robert Dollar wrote in his memoirs, "and the rent of $15-a-month includes water, electricity and wood."[21] The houses were designed by his wife, Margaret. The small village, known as "Dollarton," had a post office, a church and a school, as well as bunkhouses for the single men. The area was isolated and most people came and went by boat until the Dollarton Highway opened in the early 1930s, linking Roche Point to North Vancouver and the "outside world." The highway was built, in part, as a work project for local men who needed employment during the Depression, which brought hard times for the forest industry. After years of prosperity, the Cedarside Mill closed, followed by the larger Dollar Mill in 1942. Jobs grew scarce and many people had to leave Dollarton.

Wartime

When World War II broke out in September 1939, North Vancouver was far from the front lines. Nonetheless the war had a deep impact on the community. Initially there was anxiety around the Lower Mainland about a possible enemy attack from across the Pacific, a fear that intensified with the air assault on the American naval base at Pearl Harbor in Hawaii in December 1941. Early the next year the federal government ordered the forced evacuation of all Japanese-Canadian residents from coastal British Columbia, whether they were Canadian citizens or not. Their property was seized and they were removed to internment camps in the Interior or sent to live in other provinces. Japanese families in North Vancouver were among the victims of this shameful episode in Canadian history.

Opposite top: The Air Raid Precautions firefighting unit in Lynn Valley with its fire truck, a converted Stutz two-seater touring car, towing a pump. NVMA 726

Opposite bottom: Members of the Canadian Women's Training Corps during an exercise at Mahon Park sponsored by the ARP in May 1941. NVMA 9416

A.R.P
CIVIL DEFENCE
POST 67
LYNN VALLEY

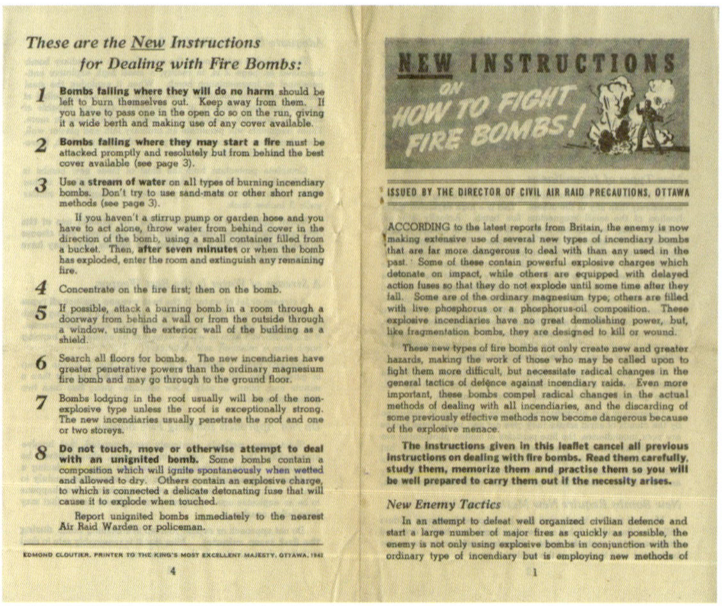

These are the New Instructions for Dealing with Fire Bombs:

1 **Bombs falling where they will do no harm** should be left to burn themselves out. Keep away from them. If you have to pass one in the open do so on the run, giving it a wide berth and making use of any cover available.

2 **Bombs falling where they may start a fire** must be attacked promptly and resolutely but from behind the best cover available (see page 3).

3 Use a **stream of water** on all types of burning incendiary bombs. Don't try to use sand-mats or other short range methods (see page 3).

If you haven't a stirrup pump or garden hose and you have to act alone, throw water from behind cover in the direction of the bomb, using a small container filled from a bucket. Then, **after seven minutes** or when the bomb has exploded, enter the room and extinguish any remaining fire.

4 Concentrate on the fire first; then on the bomb.

5 If possible, attack a burning bomb in a room through a doorway from behind a wall or from the outside through a window, using the exterior wall of the building as a shield.

6 Search all floors for bombs. The new incendiaries have greater penetrative powers than the ordinary magnesium fire bomb and may go through to the ground floor.

7 Bombs lodging in the roof usually will be of the non-explosive type unless the roof is exceptionally strong. The new incendiaries usually penetrate the roof and one or two storeys.

8 **Do not touch, move or otherwise attempt to deal with an unignited bomb.** Some bombs contain a composition which will ignite spontaneously when wetted and allowed to dry. Others contain an explosive charge, to which is connected a delicate detonating fuse that will cause it to explode when touched.

Report unignited bombs immediately to the nearest Air Raid Warden or policeman.

EDMOND CLOUTIER, PRINTER TO THE KING'S MOST EXCELLENT MAJESTY, OTTAWA, 1942

4

NEW INSTRUCTIONS ON HOW TO FIGHT FIRE BOMBS!

ISSUED BY THE DIRECTOR OF CIVIL AIR RAID PRECAUTIONS, OTTAWA

ACCORDING to the latest reports from Britain, the enemy is now making extensive use of several new types of incendiary bombs that are far more dangerous to deal with than any used in the past. Some of these contain powerful explosive charges which detonate on impact, while others are equipped with delayed action fuses so that they do not explode until some time after they fall. Some are of the ordinary magnesium type; others are filled with live phosphorus or a phosphorus-oil composition. These explosive incendiaries have no great demolishing power, but, like fragmentation bombs, they are designed to kill or wound.

These new types of fire bombs not only create new and greater hazards, making the work of those who may be called upon to fight them more difficult, but necessitate radical changes in the general tactics of defence against incendiary raids. Even more important, these bombs compel radical changes in the actual methods of dealing with all incendiaries, and the discarding of some previously effective methods now become dangerous because of the explosive menace.

The instructions given in this leaflet cancel all previous instructions on dealing with fire bombs. Read them carefully, study them, memorize them and practise them so you will be well prepared to carry them out if the necessity arises.

New Enemy Tactics

In an attempt to defeat well organized civilian defence and start a large number of major fires as quickly as possible, the enemy is not only using explosive bombs in conjunction with the ordinary type of incendiary but is employing new methods of

1

Above: Students wearing gas masks flee from Queen Mary School during an emergency wartime drill. The whole of the Lower Mainland was on alert for a possible enemy invasion, especially early in the war. NVMA 732

Fear of invasion also led to the creation of a local Air Raid Precautions (ARP) unit, a group of volunteers who helped with homefront preparedness. Among their responsibilities was to ensure that residents obeyed the periodic blackouts that were imposed. When an air-raid siren mounted at Carisbrooke Park sounded a warning, all homes and businesses were expected to turn out their lights and blacken their windows. As well, street lights and traffic signals were extinguished.

Helmet, arm band and canteen belonging to an Air Raid Precautions unit volunteer. ARP was created at the outbreak of World War II, when fear of an air attack by the Japanese was widespread. Clockwise from top: NVMA 1979.140.7; NVMA 1994.52.4; NVMA 1974.104.2. Shawn McDonald photos

Down on the waterfront directly beneath the Lions Gate Bridge, the military erected an artillery emplacement as part of the defensive installations to guard the Vancouver port. A battery of guns, supported by searchlights, was installed in a three-storey concrete gantry and manned round the clock by members of the 15th Coast Brigade of the militia. Known as "Narrows North," this gun tower, along with a similar emplacement at Ferguson Point in Stanley Park, was expected to repel any attempt by enemy craft to enter the harbour. As it turned out, the attack never came and the installation was abandoned as soon as Japan surrendered in August 1945.

On the bright side, the war brought a return to better economic times on the North Shore, largely because of the shipbuilding industry. As a result of the demand for ships from North Vancouver's two shipyards, there was a huge expansion in the workforce. At the height of the construction boom, for example, more than fourteen thousand men and women worked at Burrard Dry Dock in three shifts running around the clock seven days a week. The ferries were so crowded with commuters pouring across the inlet to work that extra vessels had to be put into service. In the autumn of 1942, as more and more men were called away to fight in the war, the company became the first shipbuilder in Canada to hire significant numbers of women to work in the yards. (That said, most of these women lost their jobs at the end of the war when men returned from the fighting.)

During the war, women took on many of the skilled jobs once done only by men. These women are working in the Burrard Dry Dock electrical department in 1945. NVMA 27–77

Marie Desimone worked as a rivet passer in the shipyard. NVMA 15767

Shortly before the end of the war in 1945 the female employees at Burrard Dry Dock posed in the yard, proud of the contribution they had made to the war effort.
NVMA 1421. Sign: NVMA INV1032

BOILERMAKERS' & IRON SHIPBUILDERS' UNION OF CANADA
SHOP
STEWARD
LOCAL No. 1

Above: Victory ships under construction at Burrard Dry Dock in 1945. The Victory class were large cargo vessels used to carry supplies from North America to an embattled Europe. NVMA 27–2289

Opposite: Phyllis Plume (l.) and Maria Bouvier were two of the women who worked at Burrard Dry Dock building ships during the war. NVMA 9613

> "I have never regretted ever working in the shipyards. My mother was horrified to think that I was wearing men's pants! Not me. I can still hear my mother: 'Eileen, you wouldn't!' I said, 'Oh yes, I would!'"
> —Eileen Doherty, first female employee at Burrard Dry Dock[22]

Many commuters would have preferred to live close to their place of work, but North Vancouver, like many other places in Canada, had a shortage of affordable housing. During the tough times of the Depression, people were giving up their homes, not building new ones. Then, with the outbreak of war, a flood of workers into urban areas placed enormous pressure on housing stocks. The federal government responded to the housing shortage by creating a crown agency, Wartime Housing Limited (WHL), to build and manage inexpensive housing for war workers. Between 1941 and 1944, WHL built more than seventeen thousand houses and other assorted buildings across Canada. In North Vancouver the agency built hundreds of single-family bungalows, primarily in the City around the western edge of Moodyville and in Lower Lonsdale close to the shipyards. But there was also development at the edge of the District, in the flatlands near Mackay Creek known as "Skunk Hollow" (the site of today's Capilano Mall). The compact, one-storey houses, which rented for twenty-two to thirty dollars per month, were supposed to be a temporary solution to the housing crunch and were intended to be removed, though many survived into the postwar period.

Left: Some of the wartime bungalows were built in Skunk Hollow, shown here, a low-lying area south of Marine Drive, approximately where Capilano Mall is now located. NVMA 10996

Right: This was one of the typical four-bedroom bungalows built as wartime housing for shipyard workers by the federal government. NVMA 3420

A collection of Burrard Dry Dock employee badges. Each of the thousands of employees had a number linked to his or her time card, pay packet and any other company record. NVMA 1992.40.2111 Shawn McDonald photo

"We used to save things like bacon fat—keep it in a tin in the refrigerator and accumulate it. And up at 14th and Lonsdale there was the Nova Theatre and two blocks up was the Lonsdale Theatre. And they would often have war drives. So on Saturday afternoons, usually it was a cowboy picture or maybe a serial—I remember the *Mark of Zorro* and things like that. But your admission was bringing a tin of bacon fat, a jam tin full. Another item was to roll up the foil from cigarette packages, any household foil, and make a ball and if it was the size of a six-inch ball that too could be brought and you'd get admission to the Saturday afternoon show."

—Murray Dykeman, former District mayor, on his wartime boyhood[23]

The Lonsdale Theatre (1920s), where generations of youngsters went to the Saturday pictures, was located on Lonsdale Avenue from 1911 to its closure in 1954. The building was later a bank, then demolished in 1997. NVMA 6344

Postwar Boom

Following World War II, the North Shore experienced an explosion of demand for reasonably priced housing. Now that access to Vancouver was assured with the opening and reopening of bridges at both the First and Second Narrows during the 1930s, large tracts of land opened for residential development. Prior to the war, North Vancouver had been a suburb of Vancouver; after the war it came of age as a community in its own right. "Returning veterans, a pent-up demand for cheap housing, the baby boom, ready availability of automobiles, and new consumer confidence all contributed to unprecedented growth," writes heritage consultant and historian Donald Luxton.[24] One sign of this transition was the conversion of the public transit system from "rails to rubber." After forty years of service, the BC Electric

This satellite view of North Vancouver from Indian Arm almost to the Lions Gate Bridge shows the urban area merging into the mountain wilderness beyond.
Courtesy of the District of North Vancouver

The log cabin office of Service Realty at the corner of Edgemont Boulevard and Ridgewood Drive selling lots in the postwar Capilano Highlands development.
NVMA 13080

Railway Company, with the approval of a public plebiscite, phased out its street railway service and replaced the trams with buses. Rails were lifted, roads repaved, and on April 23, 1947, the last trolley car made its final scheduled run. In the decade between 1941 and 1951, the population of the District increased by 144 percent, reaching 14,469, just slightly less than the City population of 15,687. By 1961 the population had more than doubled again (to 38,971) and the census showed that, for the first time, more people were living in the District than in the City.

Many of the North Shore's now well-established neighbourhoods date from this postwar growth period. In the central part of the District, Lynn Valley had previously been characterized by a pattern of widely scattered homes with few areas of continuous settlement. Beginning in the 1950s more and more of the forest land gave way to suburban development, compact neighbourhoods of single-family homes, centred on the commercial crossroads at the intersection of Mountain Highway and Lynn Valley Road. That intersection is where Westlynn Mall opened for business in 1971. A good example of the suburban shopping mall that was spreading throughout the Lower Mainland at the time, Westlynn, or Lynn Valley Centre

Top: Westlynn Mall, now Lynn Valley Centre, shortly after it opened in 1971. The ski slopes of Grouse Mountain are in the background. NVMA 11202

Bottom: Workers leaving the shipyard at the end of a shift in August 1957. The Pipe Shop, shown here, still stands in the heritage shipyard precinct at the foot of Lonsdale Avenue. NVMA 10431

Above: The mascot's headgear for North Vancouver High School, where the boys' sports teams were known as the Norsemen. The school was founded in 1910 and was the only high school in North Vancouver until 1957. NVMA 1983.12.35 Shawn McDonald photo

Left: This giant wooden salmon was featured at the annual employee fishing derby sponsored by the Burrard Dry Dock company during the 1950s and 1960s. NVMA 2013.INV.708

as it is now called, featured a collection of inward-facing shops surrounded by a large parking lot, much in the style of West Vancouver's Park Royal, which had pioneered the style when it opened in 1950 as Canada's first shopping mall.

Lynn Valley retained a working-class identity through the 1960s. Perhaps because of its history as a logging community, perhaps because of its location a bit removed from the central core, "the Valley" was known as a blue-collar enclave in a wider community that was fast becoming middle-class. "Lynn Valley," recalls Bob McCormack, who grew up there in the 1950s, "was lunch bucket. Burrard Dry Dock, the King Lumber Company. People came home on a Friday night with soot and dirt all over them. So I think the culture was such that we didn't have a lot."[25] The Valley also was known for its youth gangs, whose members hung out on the streets, drank and committed various forms of mayhem. The Ant Hill Mob and the Smiling Crabs were two of the more oddly named of the gangs, which other teens gave a wide berth. It was all pretty innocent by modern standards, but at the time, they added to the Valley's rough-hewn reputation, which began to fade during the 1970s as all the neighbourhoods on the North Shore started to lose their distinct identities and merge into a shared "North Vancouverness."

The Stardust Roller Rink on West 14th Street, a teen hangout from 1964 until its closure in 1983. NVMA item 1179–4

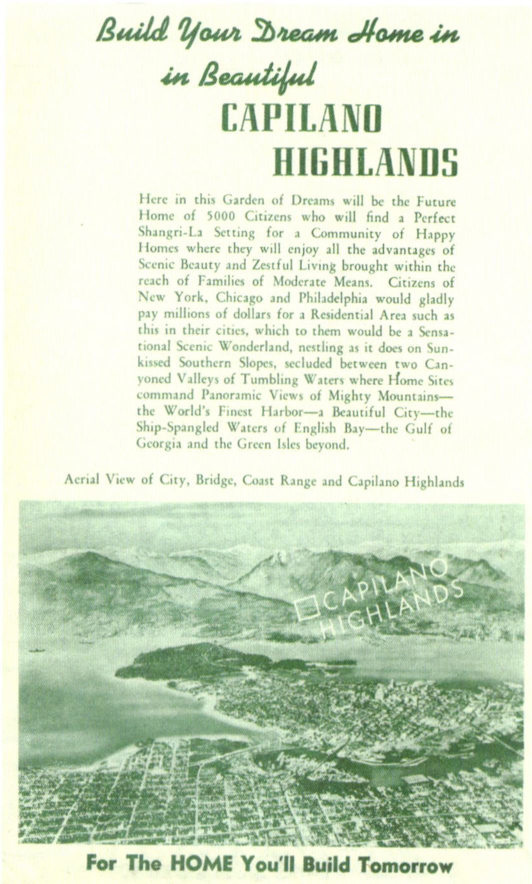

"As a teenager, going to Balmoral and then Carson Graham [in the 1960s] there were the boys from my neighbourhood [Edgemont] and there were the Valley boys and they were a different breed for sure. They were considered tougher . . . The Valley had a real distinct . . . you know, if you were from the Valley you were considered to be tough."
—Terri Johnson[26]

Farther west, another of the postwar subdivisions was Capilano Highlands, located between the Capilano River and Mosquito Creek. Although the plan for this development dates from before the war, it did not get underway until the immediate postwar period. The development featured the work of noted architect Fred Hollingsworth, who had his own home in the area and designed the street layout and many residences in the Highlands. The commercial hub of the neighbourhood became known as "Edgemont Village," which continues to be a busy business and shopping centre. The last major residential

Top: Sowden Street in the Norgate neighbourhood, ca. 1950. Norgate was a post-war subdivision characterized by smaller homes built in assembly-line fashion. NVMA 572

Above left: This postcard, dated 1969, illustrates the suburban ideal of a single-family residence, a green lawn and an automobile in the driveway that propelled the optimistic postwar development of North Vancouver. NVMA 15980

Above right: The "Trend House" on Skyline Drive was one of the featured homes in Capilano Highlands. Completed in 1954, it was one of eleven houses built across Canada to showcase the use of wood in modern construction. VPL 82529A

THE ARCHITECT OF EDGEMONT

Fred Hollingsworth was born in England in 1917 and came to Canada as a teenager with his parents. He graduated from high school in Vancouver in the middle of the Depression. Jobs were hard to find and young Fred apprenticed as a sheet metal worker. During World War II he worked at Vancouver's Boeing Aircraft plant. He was also an accomplished jazz saxophonist, leading his own dance band for several years.

Following the war, Hollingsworth and his wife, Phyllis, purchased a lot in Capilano Highlands, where he designed his own home. Impressed by the design, Ned Pratt offered him a job as a draftsman at his renowned architectural firm, Thompson Berwick and Pratt. TBP nurtured many of the masters of West Coast Modernism, including Arthur Erickson, Ron Thom, Geoff Massey and Barry Downs. The style was characterized by the plentiful use of wood and glass, flat roofs with large overhangs, open interior floor plans and an attempt to integrate the structure with its surrounding landscape.

Impressed by Hollingsworth's talent, the developer of Capilano Highlands, Eric Allan, asked him to design many of the modern homes that characterized the new neighbourhood. One of these, the so-called "Sky Bungalow," was installed in the parking lot of the Hudson's Bay Company store downtown as a show home for the development. Capilano Highlands became known as "Hollingsworth's Oak Park," a reference to the Chicago-area village famous for its many buildings designed by Frank Lloyd Wright.

Hollingsworth became a certified architect in 1959 and eventually set up his own practice, for many years located in the home that he had designed for himself near Edgemont Village, where he lived until his death in 2015.

development in the Highlands took place in the 1980s in Grousewoods, near the lower terminal of the Grouse Mountain Skyride.

Closer to the waterfront and the Lions Gate Bridge, the flatland now known as "Norgate" was initially cleared in 1947 as the site for a small airport. When the airport plan fell through, the land was sold to a developer and, by 1952, five hundred houses had been built, each with the identical floorplan, though exterior design features varied. Each house sold for nine thousand dollars. The first high-rises anywhere in the District were built in the Lower Capilano area in the 1970s, at Woodcroft on the banks of the river and at the International Plaza on Marine Drive.

Following World War II the eastern end of the District also rallied. The site of the abandoned Dollar mill was subdivided into lots for the Roslyn Park subdivision. Shipbuilders located along the waterfront. Among the most prominent was Sam Matsumoto. After being interned in Slocan during the war as part of the displacement of Japanese from the coast, Matsumoto settled in Dollarton where he opened Matsumoto and Sons Shipyard in 1949. Specializing in aluminum vessels, Matsumoto manufactured the first

The Matsumoto shipyard specialized in aluminum fishing boats, like the gillnetters shown here on the ways in 1961. VPL 45901

aluminum-welded boats in North America. The yard was sold in 1988 to Allied Shipbuilders. Even earlier than Matsumoto, Mackenzie Barge and Marine Ways built marine vessels and carried out ship repairs on the Dollarton Highway from 1932. Both these yards have been bulldozed to make way for new residential developments.

Around the corner from Roche Point, Deep Cove transitioned from a summer cottage community into a suburban neighbourhood in the postwar period. With improved road access, more people settled permanently and by 1961 the Cove had a population in excess of four hundred. District government began to take more of an interest in the community. In 1970 the municipality took over the land where the dance hall and a motel had been and turned it into a waterfront park. Residents of the Cove have worked to accommodate the inevitable changes that development

Deep Cove's "main street," Gallant Avenue, in the 1960s. NVMA 106–10–11

brings with the desire to retain a village atmosphere for their community.

Between Deep Cove and the Seymour River a series of residential subdivisions gradually filled in both sides of the Mount Seymour Parkway (the modern name for that section of Keith Road). The Blueridge, Seymour Heights and Windsor Park neighbourhoods all expanded during this period, facilitated by the completion of the new Second Narrows Bridge in 1960 and the opening of the Upper Levels Highway between the bridge and West Vancouver early in 1961. By the late 1980s the growth of the Parkgate area led to plans for a neighbourhood centre near the entrance to Seymour Provincial Park. These plans, which came to fruition during the following decade, included a shopping centre (Parkgate, which opened in 1992), a branch library (1995) and a community centre (1999). Northlands Golf Course, owned and operated by the District, opened for 18-hole play in 1997. In the context of the District as a whole, the Seymour area, both west and east, has experienced the most growth in population since the 1980s.

Construction of the bridge across the Capilano River was part of the completion of the Upper Levels Highway between the river and the Ironworkers Memorial Bridge in 1961. The project cut through the centre of the District. NVMA 3604

During the mid-1990s, developments east of the Seymour prompted a spirited public backlash when it was announced that the District had plans to sell public forest lands along the lower flanks of Mount Seymour for residential construction. Local residents wanted this area, which was widely used by hikers and mountain bikers, preserved as parkland, and they organized to oppose development. A petition calling for a halt to the project attracted more than ten thousand signatures. The result was that the District council rezoned the contested areas, known as Mountain Forest and Cove Forest, as recreational. This protest indicated that many residents were determined to preserve the identity of the District as a "green" community that protected its natural environment. The policy of selling off wilderness land

Left: When Park Royal opened in September 1950 on the north side of Marine Drive in West Vancouver, it was the first shopping mall in Canada. NVMA 4051

to finance public facilities was brought into question, along with the rapid pace of residential development.

In contrast to the expansive developments in the District, in the City the Lower Lonsdale neighbourhood fell on hard times during the 1950s. A number of factors contributed to this stagnation. Following the closure of the streetcars in 1947 and the cessation of ferry service to downtown Vancouver in 1958, the area ceased to be the transportation hub it had been. Thousands of commuters no longer passed through the neighbourhood each day on their way to and from work and shopping. Instead they drove across the bridges. Local businesses felt the crunch. The shipyards no longer employed as many people, and the opening of Park Royal shopping centre in West Vancouver drew away customers from local shops. What had been the commercial heart of the North Shore was beating only faintly, while farther north a new civic centre emerged in the mid-1970s with the construction of a modern city hall, library and fire hall in the Central Lonsdale area.

Civic officials recognized the need to revitalize Lower Lonsdale. The arrival of the SeaBus in 1977 was a big help. Once again a "ferry" connected the North Shore to Vancouver and the bottom of Lonsdale regained its strategic location as a transportation centre.

In 1979 the city partnered with the province to develop the waterfront with the construction of Lonsdale Quay and neighbouring Waterfront Park. As part of the development, the Insurance Company of BC (ICBC) located its new headquarters nearby and the province established the Pacific Marine Training Institute. When the Quay opened in 1985 the complex included a public market, a hotel, office towers, condominiums and a bus depot. It was a terrific shot in the arm for a neighbourhood that looked to be getting back on its feet.

NVMA 1985-24

Above: The opening of the Quay, and the development of Lower Lonsdale that it spearheaded, led to the designation of the Lonsdale Corridor as one of nine regional city centres in Greater Vancouver. NVMA 160-429. Bruce Flanagan photo

Below: Aerial view of a revived Lower Lonsdale neighbourhood. Lisa Wilson photo

Meanwhile the historic Versatile Pacific Shipyards was entering its final days. When it closed in 1992—the dry dock at the eastern end of the site was saved and is now operated by Seaspan—it left a broad swath of waterfront land vacant. In 2001 Pinnacle International won the right to develop the land, and a new hotel and a series of residential towers was built as a first step in revitalizing this stretch of waterfront. In 2014 City council rebranded the site "The Shipyards" and plans moved forward to develop part of it as a public gathering spot. After thirty years of development, Lower Lonsdale, with its ferry dock, public market, forest of new high-rise residential towers and heritage precinct, is set to become a gateway to the new North Shore.

"When I was first elected in 1993, Lower Lonsdale was not a nice place. You know, it was where beer parlours were and vast open parking lots and abandoned buildings, and the shipyards were closed. It was not a nice place. The SeaBus was a bit of an anomaly. When that opened in 1977, and Lonsdale Quay, that kind of looked to potential, and with the ICBC moving in, it started bringing some people in. It said, 'Hey, we have some potential here.' So through the 1980s, they started to plan that, and then in the 1990s we actually started to build residential in Lower Lonsdale, and it's been very successful ever since."
—City mayor Darrell Mussatto[27]

An aerial view of the North Vancouver waterfront ca. 1977 shows a completed SeaBus terminal, the site of Lonsdale Quay to the right and the future Waterfront Park to the left. NVMA 9287

CRACKING THE POLITICAL GLASS CEILING

While Vancouverites have never elected a woman to be their mayor, voters in the City of North Vancouver opted for a female leader way back in the 1960s. The first local politician to break through the gender barrier, Carrie Cates, served a single term as alderman and then won election three times as City mayor, serving from 1964 to 1969. Next, District voters took their turn. In 1982 they chose Marilyn Baker as mayor; she held the position for the next eight years. The trend continued in 1999 when Barbara Sharp was sworn in to the first of two terms as City mayor, followed in 2004/05 by Janice Harris in the District.

Above: Marilyn Baker (r.), the District's first female mayor, poses with the statue of Walter Draycott, and Kevin Head, the artist who sculpted it, in Pioneer Park in 1986. NVMA 6743

Top right: Carrie Cates, the first woman elected mayor of either municipality on the North Shore. She served from 1964 to 1969. NVMA 4830

POPULATION CHART—CITY AND DISTRICT

Year	City	District
1901	365	
1911	8,196	
1921	7,652	2,950
1951	15,687	14,469
1971	31,847	57,861
2001	43,925	82,310
2011	48,196	84,412

An Alternative Lifestyle

While middle-class residential neighbourhoods were emerging after the war, there was an alternative form of housing meant for the less well-to-do—squatters' cabins. Historically, these makeshift dwellings were located on the foreshore at several locations around Burrard Inlet. Sizeable squatter communities were located in Stanley Park, Coal Harbour, False Creek, Brighton Beach and east of the Second Narrows at "Crabtown" in Burnaby. Often constructed of driftwood or scraps from the lumber mills, they stood on stilts and were usually "off the grid," having neither electricity nor plumbing. Often the dwellings belonged

One of the Dollarton-area squatter's shacks. Living "off the grid" around the shores of Burrard Inlet was once a common lifestyle for artists, bohemians, recluses and anyone who just needed a cheap place to live. NVMA 8602

Top: Scale replicas of squatters' shacks by Vancouver artist Ken Lum are installed at the Maplewood Conservation Area. Lisa Wilson photo

Above left and right: This blue cabin was the last of the squatter cabins that once dotted the shoreline of the North Shore. Occupied for many years by Vancouver artists Al Neil and Carole Itter, it was moved in 2015. Michael McCarthy photos

Top: The squatter community at Maplewood Flats. Residents were burned out in the early 1970s and eventually the site became a wildlife conservation area. Vladimir Keremidschieff/Vancouver Sun

Above left: Squatters at their cabins in July 1971, shortly before they were evicted. George Diack/Vancouver Sun

Above right: Squatters watch while their cabins burn, December 1971. Dan Scott/Vancouver Sun to single men—fishermen, beachcombers, hermits, pensioners, workers at nearby mills and boatyards—but there were families as well. The cabins were especially attractive to free-spirited, artistic types who didn't have a lot of money and didn't mind the lack of secure tenure. It has been estimated that they provided homes to as many as 1,800 people in the inlet during the 1930s and 1940s, but during the 1950s port authorities razed almost all of them.

On the North Shore, squatter communities appeared at Roche Point and Maplewood Flats. The one at Roche Point, sometimes called "Lazy Bay," began during the depressed economic times of the 1930s and numbered about ninety structures at its height. It was notable as the centre of a bohemian community of poets and painters that included, at one time or another, the poets Dorothy Livesay and Earle Birney. The most famous of the literary residents was the British-born novelist Malcolm Lowry, who lived at the point with his wife Margerie Bonner from 1940 to 1954. Most of his best-known novel, *Under the Volcano*, was written there. The ramshackle Roche Point dwellings were bulldozed in the late 1950s, though one or two survived, and the area became Cates Park.

At Maplewood Flats at the mouth of McCartney Creek, a small squatter community associated with the hippy counterculture occupied several shacks and tents in the late 1960s. The District government burned down these dwellings in the early 1970s, ostensibly to make way for a shopping mall that never materialized. The one exception was a home belonging to an elderly resident who was allowed to remain until 1986, when he went into a nursing home and his shack was demolished. The last squatter's home at Roche Point—indeed, the last in Burrard Inlet—belonged to the jazz musician and poet Al Neil and his co-resident, the artist Carole Itter. Neil worked for many years as a watchman for the boatyard next door, but in 2015, he and Itter were evicted by the Port Authority to make way for redevelopment of the waterfront and their cabin was relocated. It was the official end of a colourful era.

Tom Burrows, an artist and Maplewood resident, with his son Elisha at their cabin on the Flats, December 1971. Ken Oakes/Vancouver Sun

Re-amalgamation

The City and the District of North Vancouver became separate municipalities in 1907, but the possibility of re-amalgamation has never been far from the minds of North Shore residents who wonder whether their relatively small geographic area requires two governments. During the period when local government was suspended, Commissioner Charles Tisdall thought that re-amalgamation would save money by avoiding the duplication of public services. In 1939 water commissioner E. A. Cleveland proposed the creation of a single, smaller municipality focused on the lower slopes, with everything to the north becoming provincial parkland. The *Vancouver Sun* concurred. "Could not city and municipality join in a new shore-line corporation," the newspaper asked in a July 15 editorial, "running back only to the foot of the mountains?" Despite apparent support among local business leaders, the idea was not acted upon, probably because of the outbreak of World War II.

During the 1950s, in part because of the troubled financial situation of the prewar period, local politicians again began to consider reuniting the two municipalities. In 1957 the City commissioned a study of the financial implications of a merger, but despite concluding that it made economic sense, council did not pursue it. Almost ten years later, two separate studies concluded

This cartoon by David Alavoine in the North Shore Citizen pokes fun at the issue of amalgamation. The caption reads: "Your father's chairman of tonight's meeting on 'Communities in Harmony and Amalgamation'!" NVMA David Alavoine Fonds 185

COOPERATING FOR HEALTH

Lions Gate Hospital is another example of municipal cooperation on the North Shore. It traces its origins back to May 1908 when a small, six-bed hospital opened in a private home near East 15th Street and St. Andrews Avenue. The North Vancouver Hospital (NVH) was owned and operated by three sisters, all of whom were nurses trained in England: Mina and Jenny Dawson and their married sister, Margaret Stevenson.

Just two years later, the NVH moved to slightly larger premises with fifteen beds, located on East 12th Street. It was also owned by the Dawsons. Failing health led to the sisters' retirement, and early in 1921, the District of North Vancouver purchased the building and added a new wing. This facility was the first publicly owned hospital on the North Shore. Interestingly, it was owned and operated by the District, though it was located in the City.

As the years passed, the local medical community recognized that a larger, better equipped hospital was required. The District and the City agreed to share the cost and a new, sixty-bed North Vancouver General Hospital (NVGH) opened in May 1929 on East 13th Street.

By the 1950s the NVGH was becoming overcrowded. After years of delay, the three North Shore municipalities reached an agreement to share responsibility for a new facility, and in April 1961, the Lions Gate Hospital opened at its present location on East 13th Street and St. Georges Avenue. Expanded and renewed many times since, Lions Gate today has 268 beds and offers a wide range of general and acute care services.

Mina Dawson in 1905. She was one of the three sisters who founded the first hospital in North Vancouver.
NVMA 5549

that a single municipality would deliver services more efficiently and more cost-effectively. A case in point was the joint City/District project to commemorate Canada's upcoming one hundredth birthday in 1967. All across the country, communities were taking advantage of the centennial to sponsor their own birthday projects. Along with a host of municipal centres, parks and museums, these included a bathtub race across the Strait of Georgia and, in St. Paul, Alberta, a landing pad for flying saucers. In North Vancouver a more practical centennial committee decided on a new community recreation complex, encompassing hockey and curling rinks, a swimming pool and a civic auditorium. The public overwhelmingly endorsed the idea in a referendum, and in 1966, the North Vancouver Memorial Community Centre (now the Harry Jerome centre) and Centennial Theatre complex opened at Lonsdale and 23rd. (A Japanese tea house, constructed in 1910, had once stood on the site, along with a horticultural garden.) Shortly afterwards, in 1970, the two municipalities created a joint recreation commission to administer indoor and outdoor recreation activities.

> "So up until 1967 recreation was provided by people themselves and they had to look after it. And the municipality wasn't providing recreation facilities, not on an extensive basis. That picture started to change in 1966/67 when suddenly the District and the City together went into recreation and the whole recreation picture started to change."
> —Dirk Oostindie, District parks superintendent 1959–1993[28]

But if anyone had thought so, this was not a first step to re-amalgamation. Most members of City council, in particular Mayor Carrie Cates, were set against the idea, even when the provincial government got involved. In the spring of 1967 the Minister of Municipal Affairs, who favoured the idea of a single municipality, more or less ordered the City and District to hold a referendum on the issue, which they did in order to avoid what District Reeve Ron Andrews called "a shotgun marriage with the Provincial government holding the shotgun."[29] On September 19, 1968, North Vancouverites cast their votes on amalgamation. The result was both Yes and No. In the District, close to 90 percent of electors voted in favour, but in the City only 50.5 percent of voters approved and the law required a 60 percent approval in both municipalities. Many people observed that a minority of voters had scuttled the plan but there was nothing anyone could do. Nonetheless the issue continued to simmer and, in the spring of 1971, the City polled its residents once again on the issue. This time the vote against amalgamation was pronounced: 65 percent of voters said "No."

For the time being the issue was dormant, but it never stayed asleep for long. In 1973 the provincial government once again hinted at forcing a merger, and despite the adamant opposition of City mayor Tom Reid, the two councils established a joint committee to study the issue once again. This committee dragged on its considerations for years without ever coming to a conclusion. The possibility of re-amalgamation has been raised several times since, most recently in 2014 when the District created a North Shore Reunification Committee to investigate the issue. The committee identified a range of questions that needed answers. Would reunification bring higher taxes? Would it improve the quality of public services on the North Shore? Would it change public access to government? What would a unified political structure look like? How should public opinion on the issue be determined? And so on. While the District over the years has been in favour of at least considering reunification, officials in the City continue to believe the financial disadvantages outweigh any possible advantages. Long-time City mayor Jack Loucks put it succinctly in 1995: "We figure the city could only be a real loser in amalgamation."[30]

MAN WITH A KIND HEART

Chief Simon Baker (1911–2001), whose Squamish name, Khot-La-Cha, meant "man with a kind heart," was a fisherman, stevedore and long-time member of the Squamish Band Council. He wrote in 1994:

> I look at the Squamish Band today and see the houses, many of them even better than those owned by white people in North Vancouver. Everybody on our reserves has running water, indoor toilets, electricity. Everybody pretty well has microwave ovens, VCRS, you name it. Lots of people have modern cars, some have more than one car. This is good. I always wanted my people to have everything like the white man. We had to fight hard for those things. Young people today don't realize how us old-timers worked in them days, about fifty years ago, to get what we have today.[31]

For many years Khot-La-Cha was a respected ambassador for his people across Canada and abroad, a role that was recognized by his admission to the Order of Canada in 1997.

Diversifying the Population

One of the most important events to shape the modern character of North Vancouver did not take place on the North Shore at all. During the 1970s, far away on the other side of the world, opposition was gathering against the Pahlavi dynasty, which had ruled Iran for five decades. Demonstrations against the ruling shah paralyzed the country until finally he was forced into exile early in 1979 and Iran became an Islamic republic led by the Ayatollah Khomeini. During this turbulent period, many Iranians left the country to live abroad, whether they were supporters of the old regime or belonged to religious or ethnic minority groups and feared persecution by the new. During the 1980s the war between Iran and Iraq led others to seek a more stable life overseas. Many of these exiles were attracted to the Lower Mainland, and in particular to the North Shore, which resembles the mountainous area around Tehran. The initially small community of newcomers attracted others who desired to settle among friends and relatives, until by 2012, there were close to eleven thousand Farsi-speaking people living on the North Shore. Their community is very diverse both religiously and ethnically, and includes Muslims, Christians, Sufis, Zoroastrians, Baha'is, Kurds, Turks and Armenians. Their presence is reflected in the variety of Persian-oriented merchants on Lonsdale Avenue, the celebration of Persian festivals and the proliferation of Farsi media.

Iranians are just one immigrant group among many that contributed to the diversification and the growth of the North Vancouver population from the 1970s onward. In 1972 the dictator Idi Amin expelled people of Asian descent from Uganda. Among the eighty thousand exiles were many Ismaili Muslims. For the first

Iranian newcomers have contributed in many ways to the culture and economy of North Vancouver since the 1970s. Clockwise from top: Members of the Atash Dance Troupe, a group founded by Mojdeh Shahriari in 1990 (NVMA photo)**. Nassreen Filsoof of the Canadian Iranian Foundation preparing for the celebration of Nowruz, the Iranian New Year** (NVMA photo)**. Vanak Market and Deli on Lonsdale Avenue.** (Michael Fortney photo).

Above: Pars International Food is located on the 100 block of West 16th near other food outlets and restaurants popular with the Persian community. Cecil Halsey photo

Left: The Nava Arts Centre was incorporated in 2003 by musician Hossein Behroozinia (l.) as a cultural centre for learning and performing fine arts. Cecil Halsey photo

Top and above right: Members of the Yada family, shown outside their grocery store at East 4th Street and Queensbury Avenue, and on an outing in 1921, owned their business from 1904 until they were interned in 1942 and lost everything. Top: NVMA 9532; above right: NVMA 9533

Above left: Lim Gong, shown outside his Lower Lonsdale store, arrived in North Vancouver in 1900 and opened this grocery, which thrived for many years. He died in 1951 at 85 years of age. CVA P354 time Canada agreed to accept a substantial number of refugees from a non-European country. Of the 5,700 who came, most were Ismailis, many of whom settled on the North Shore. Despite being allowed to bring almost nothing when they left Uganda, they quickly adapted to life in their new home. In 1992 the community opened the Headquarters-Lion's Gate Jamatkhana, a spiritual and social centre located near Murdo Frazer Park, designed by noted Ismaili architect Farouk Noormohamed. All these newcomers—Iranian, Ismaili and others—faced many of the same challenges encountered by most immigrants to a new country. Accommodations in North Vancouver were expensive and not all the newcomers were well off. Jobs were hard to come by, especially for those lacking a proficiency in English. Professional people—lawyers, doctors, engineers—often did not have their qualifications recognized. Yet despite these impediments, most immigrants were able to make a successful transition to life in their new home.

According to the Canadian census, the population of the District had become 22 percent visible minority by 2011, slightly less than the provincial level of 24 percent but considerably more diversified than it had been even twenty years earlier. In the same year the City population was 29 percent visible minority.

2011 VISIBLE MINORITY POPULATION—CITY AND DISTRICT

	District	City
Total population	84,412	48,196
Total visible minority	18,380	13,915
Chinese	4,660	1,825
South Asian	2,245	1,475
Black	235	390
Filipino	1,855	3,335
Latin American	790	585
Southeast Asian	430	135
Arab	180	235
West Asian	4,500	3,420
Korean	1,645	1,210
Japanese	1,250	740
Others	140	55
Multiple	455	520

Source: Welcome BC

THE JEROMES, NORTH VANCOUVER'S RECORD SETTERS

At one time during the 1960s, North Vancouver was home to the fastest person on the planet. Harry Jerome arrived with his family from Winnipeg in 1952, when he was twelve years old. The Jeromes, a black family, endured the prejudice that was typical of the day; Harry's younger sister, Valerie, recalls the other children throwing rocks at the Jerome kids on the first day of school. But it wasn't long before Harry's athletic talent was recognized. As a teenage track star he first broke the high school record for the 220-yard sprint. Then, a year later, he tied the world record of 10 seconds flat for the 100-metre dash. Harry represented Canada at two Pan-American Games and two Commonwealth Games, where he turned in gold-medal performances. And at the 1964 Summer Olympics in Tokyo, he captured the bronze medal in the 100 metres. By the time he retired, he had held several world records at different distances. In 2001, almost twenty years after his premature death by a brain aneurysm, the recreation complex on Lonsdale Avenue was renamed in his honour.

A bronze statue of Jerome stands near the seawall in Stanley Park. Next to it is a bench dedicated to Valerie, who also represented Canada at the Olympics. Valerie was a standout sprinter and long jumper, and in 1960, at just sixteen years old, she joined Harry at the Summer Olympics in Rome, where she competed in the 100-metre sprint and relay. After she became a teacher in Vancouver, Valerie continued to be involved in track as an official and was an activist in the Green Party.

Herry Jerome and his sister Valerie training for the Summer Olympics in Rome in 1960, where they both competed for Canada. NVMA 14861

First Nations Revival

As North Vancouver welcomed more immigrants, the original inhabitants experienced a renewal of their culture and economic prospects. First Nations' reserve lands were supposed to be inviolable, but for years, local governments had hoped to get their hands on at least some of the land for their own purposes. Prior to World War I, for example, North Vancouver asked the federal government if it could buy the Capilano and Mission reserves so that the land could be used for port-related industry. Small pieces of the reserves were hacked off, usually without consultation with the First Nations, to accommodate the construction of Marine Drive and the Lions Gate Bridge, as well as railway rights-of-way close to the waterfront.

In the spring of 1939, King George VI and his wife, Elizabeth, paid a six-week visit to Canada, during which they spent a day in Vancouver. After touring the city in a convertible limousine and attending a luncheon at the Hotel Vancouver, the royal couple got back in their car and set off for the North Shore.

Members of the Capilano Reserve band gather on the steps of the Department of Indian Affairs building in downtown Vancouver, 1921. The band was formed in 1886 and performed at many public events. NVMA 4834

Canoe racing was an important tradition for the Squamish and Tsleil-Waututh First Nations. This photograph shows racing at the Mission Reserve in 1962. VPL 85811L

NVMA 1952-2

They crossed the Second Narrows Bridge and drove westward through both the City and the District, acknowledging the cheers of tens of thousands of people, many of them schoolchildren, who lined the route. On their way to the Lions Gate Bridge the royals passed by the Capilano Reserve, where the Squamish people had asked to meet them. But the procession was running late and the car did not stop. Mary Agnes Capilano, then one hundred years old, was sorely disappointed not to be able to speak to the queen. Later, an official of the royal visit committee wrote to the Band: "We are assured that Their Majesties took particular pains to acknowledge the homage of their Indian subjects, and that in passing them the rate of speed was considerably lowered."[32] The disappointment of the royal visit seemed to symbolize the indifference with which officialdom then treated the local First Nations.

In 1899 the Oblate brothers, Catholic missionaries who had great influence amongst the Squamish people, opened a residential school on Keith Road, just north of the Mission Reserve. The school, St. Paul's, staffed by a French religious order named the Sisters of the Child Jesus, was one of many boarding schools for Native children across Canada. Their sad legacy was the subject of a damning report by the Truth and Reconciliation Commission of Canada (TRC) in 2015. These schools—the last one closed in 1996—were sponsored by the federal government and operated by different religious denominations, both Catholic and Protestant. It was the intention of the schools to assimilate the Aboriginal students into mainstream society, an intention which the TRC called "cultural genocide." Aboriginal languages and cultural practices were not allowed. "There is a lot of feeling of hate about the days when people were controlled by the church and by the school," recalled Chief Simon Baker of the Mission Reserve. "At the school, they were forbidden, like at a lot of other schools, to speak the Squamish language."[33] Students, who were between the ages of three and sixteen, endured a strict routine, including regular corporal punishment and abundant religious instruction. St. Paul's, one of eighteen residential schools in British Columbia, closed in June 1959 and was demolished. In 2014 former students installed a memorial statue at the site, which is now occupied by St. Thomas Aquinas Regional Secondary School. First Nations students now attend the local public schools. As well, the Squamish Nation operates a primary school on the Capilano Reserve. Xwemelch'stn Etsimxwawtxw (Capilano Little Ones School), offers kindergarten to Grade 2 education to young members of the Nation.

> "When we went to school, really there wasn't a sense of family in that school. We all had numbers. We weren't referred to by name. And things were done on that basis because those in the school were nuns and unfortunately they never had any parenting skills. They never knew about those things that were important for us as young children growing up in that environment. I didn't sense it was family, but at nine, ten years old, something dramatic happened to me with the sisters. Two nuns had taken me out of bed and gave me one hundred on my bottom with a leather strap. One hundred. Some of my older brothers were there and they counted. And so, you know, the nuns weren't really mothers and fathers. They didn't know what it was about; it was a religious institution there, a lot of time was spent in religious instruction and praying. Unfortunately, I found out later, the sisters in that school, a number of them did not come with teaching certificates. They were learning on the job as they were going . . . So, you know, that school wasn't a real place to grow up . . ."
>
> —William Nahanee of Mission Reserve, former student of St. Paul's Indian Residential School[34]

Top: Most of the students at St. Paul's came from the Mission Reserve and other Squamish and Tsleil-Waututh communities, though some came from farther afield. This photograph shows the primary pupils in 1905. NVMA 4839

Bottom: St. Paul's Indian Residential School was located on Keith Road in North Vancouver City just north of the Mission Reserve. One of eighteen similar schools in British Columbia, it opened in 1899 and remained in operation until 1959. NVMA 11417

Badges and patches for athletic achievement at St. Paul's.
NVMA WN.067, 068, 069. Courtesy of William Nahanee

St. Paul's boxing team in the early 1950s. NVMA 4791

This small totem pole was carved by Chief Mathias Joe Capilano. The top figure is a thunderbird with outstretched wings made from a separate piece of wood.
NVMA 2014.26.1. Shawn McDonald photo

Over the years, the Squamish and the Tsleil-Waututh resisted attempts to expropriate their lands and destroy their culture. In 1923, sixteen Squamish chiefs signed an amalgamation agreement that created the Squamish Nation and established an elected council. (The Tsleil-Waututh did not join the partnership, asserting their own identity as a separate First Nation.) With time, this council took control of its own affairs from the appointed Indian agents. Many prominent leaders emerged from the North Shore reserves to defend Aboriginal rights. Dan George (Geswanouth Slahoot), chief of the Tsleil-Waututh during the 1950s and originally a longshoreman, used his position as an award-winning actor to promote the status of First Nations people. At a celebration of Canada's hundredth birthday in 1967, he stunned the crowd at Vancouver's Empire Stadium with his "Lament for Confederation," in which he rebuked Canadians for their mistreatment of Aboriginal people. Andy Paull, a former student at St. Paul's, worked in a Vancouver law office, and though First Nations were not allowed to become lawyers at the time, he was a leading spokesman on Aboriginal law and rights until his death in 1959, respected across the country for his knowledge and eloquence. Joe Mathias, who grew up on the Capilano Reserve, was a grandson of Joe Capilano. After attending law school at UBC, he served as chief of his people for many years, and was a leading Aboriginal politician with the Assembly of First Nations and other organizations.

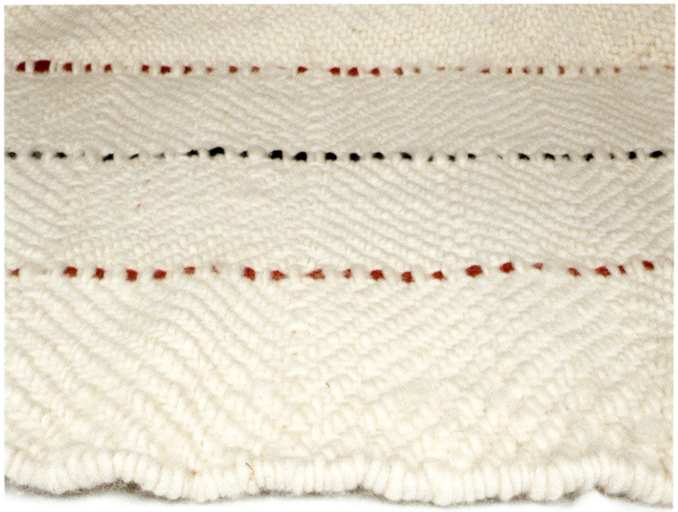

Designed and made by Keith Nahanee, this blanket (detail shown) was inspired by a historic Salish blanket. NVMA 2010.16.1 Shawn McDonald photo

Carver Alan Natrall at work on a pole. NVMA WN40. Courtesy of William Nahanee

For many years, the First Nations on the North Shore have been engaged in economic development projects to improve life in their communities. In 1992 the Tsleil-Waututh partnered with private investors to create Takaya Developments Ltd. as a vehicle for promoting economic growth. Since that time, the Nation has built several condominium and townhouse complexes on reserve land. As well, it operates a golf driving range and a canoe and kayak touring company, all under the auspices of the Takaya brand. The Squamish own the land on which part of the Park Royal Shopping Centre in West Vancouver sits, as well as a variety of other businesses.

In 1992, after many years of refusing to acknowledge Aboriginal treaty rights, the provincial government agreed to enter treaty negotiations with the First Nations, and the BC Treaty Commission was established. Both the Tsleil-Waututh and the Squamish entered the lengthy treaty process. Meanwhile, other outstanding issues were resolved. For example, in 2000 the federal government agreed to pay the Squamish Nation twenty million dollars as part of the so-called "Kitsilano Agreement." This agreement stemmed from the shameful eviction of Squamish families from their village of Snauq (the Kitsilano Indian Reserve) on Vancouver's Vanier Point in 1913. Some of these sixty to seventy people came to settle on the North Shore reserves. When restitution finally was paid in 2000, it also included lands on the North Shore that had been alienated from the Capilano and Mission reserves.

A panoramic view of the Mission Reserve in 1902. VPL 5642

Treaty agreements are one example of how the First Nations are reasserting their rights. Another is a revival of the Squamish language, which was nearly eradicated by the residential school program. A team of elders, linguists and researchers toiled for eighteen years to produce, in 2011, the *Squamish-English Dictionary*, a landmark publication containing the English equivalents for about eight thousand words in the Squamish language. The dictionary is a visible sign of the efforts the people are making to strengthen their language and culture.

> “When I fought to protect my land and my home, I was called a savage. When I neither understood nor welcomed his way of life, I was called lazy. When I tried to rule my people, I was stripped of my authority . . .
>
> Oh God! Like the thunderbird of old I shall rise again out of the sea; I shall grab the instruments of the white man's success—his education, his skills—and with these new tools I shall build my race into the proudest segment of your society.”
>
> —Chief Dan George, “Lament for Confederation”[35]

Above: These Tsimshian killer whale effigies are part of the collection of artifacts gathered by Maisie Hurley. NVMA 1986.19.92 a,b

Right: *The Native Voice*, the official publication of the Native Brotherhood of BC, began publication in 1946. This issue was dedicated to the poet Pauline Johnson on the centennial of her birth in 1861. NVMA 1961-7

ACTIVIST AND COLLECTOR

Maisie Hurley was born in Wales in 1887, and came with her parents to British Columbia when she was just a toddler. When she left school, she embarked on a colourful career as a boxing promoter and social activist. In the 1930s she went to work for the Vancouver criminal lawyer Tom Hurley, whom she later married. Together they took on many cases on behalf of the marginalized in society, including the First Nations people. In 1944 she became the first woman admitted to the Native Brotherhood of BC, and two years later she founded the *Native Voice* newspaper to advocate for Aboriginal people. When she died in 1964, many First Nations leaders felt they had lost a true friend. During her travels around North America, Maisie Hurley accumulated a significant collection of Aboriginal artifacts as gifts, now owned by the North Vancouver Museum and Archives.

Arts and Culture

At the same time as North Vancouver has become more ethnically diverse, it has also seen a proliferation of cultural institutions that reflect the maturity of the community. In 1972, for example, the North Vancouver Museum and Archives opened in the former PGE railway station, which had been moved to Mahon Park and converted for the purpose. The facility was managed by the City until 1996, when the District came on board. After four years in the cramped quarters of the railway station, the Museum and Archives moved to the Presentation House Arts Centre, a repurposed building in Lower Lonsdale that was built in 1902 as a school and then served as City Hall for sixty years. The three-storey Arts Centre also came to house the community arts council, the Presentation House Theatre and an art gallery, the Presentation House Gallery. Over the years, the venerable structure began to show its age and all three of its cultural tenants saw the need to plan for new beginnings. In 2006, the Archives moved to a new home at the Community History Centre, a renovated heritage building in Lynn Valley, while the museum continues to search for a new location. The Presentation House Gallery intends to relocate to a new facility on the waterfront next door to Lonsdale Quay, where it will contribute to the ongoing revitalization of the former shipyard lands.

Presentation House is not the only art gallery in North Vancouver. The Seymour Art Gallery has been operating in the heart of Deep Cove since 1985. Then, in 2001, the community arts council opened the CityScape Community Art Space in Lower Lonsdale as a public exhibition venue for the visual arts. It was joined in 2012 by the Gordon Smith Gallery of Canadian Art, also located on Lonsdale Avenue. In a unique collaboration, this gallery occupies the main floor of the North Vancouver School District's headquarters building, where it hosts the innovative Artists for Kids program, offering students of all ages

Top left and right: The old PGE train station during its relocation to Mahon Park in 1972, where it became the community museum. Left: NVMA 384; right: NVMA 4186.

Above: The North Vancouver Museum & Archives moved from Mahon Park (shown here) to its present location in Presentation House in 1976. NVMA 11756 the opportunity to appreciate the work of leading artists and to develop their own artistic skills. More recently, in 2015 Brigitte and Henning Freybe, art collectors and philanthropists from the North Shore, opened the Griffin Art Projects near lower Pemberton Avenue as a showcase for contemporary art.

During the 1960s the provincial government invested heavily in post-secondary education. As part of this expansion, almost a dozen two-year community colleges opened around the province. One of these was Capilano College, which began classes in temporary quarters on the grounds of West Vancouver Secondary School in September 1968. A permanent site was subsequently set aside in the Lynnmour area of the District of

capilano college communicates

PRINCIPAL'S NEWSLETTER MAY, 1971 VOLUME 3 NUMBER 8

Mobile counselling service will visit beaches, parks

Infor-m-ation will be on the move on the North Shore this summer.

This is the title given a community mobile career counselling service that will visit secondary schools, beaches, parks, street corners and other places where young people congregate.

It will be manned initially by an experienced counsellor with an extensive background in working with young people. However, if anticipated federal grants are received to finance the project, it will also be staffed by an additional 25 student assistants.

"The idea," says bearded Tim Hollick-Kenyon, director of student services at Capilano College, "is to rap with the kids on their ground providing career and other information as needed.

"You see them all summer, sitting around the beaches or the parks, with very little to do and lots of time to do it in. Some are disheartened because they cannot find jobs, others just don't know what they want to do. Often all they want is someone to talk to. They don't get much help from one another.

"Many times I have sat down on the grass at Ambleside Park and struck up a conversation with a group of young people. You would be amazed at the questions they ask. Many are really looking for help.

"The idea for Infor-m-ation — a Volkswagen bus fitted out as a travelling office — stemmed from meetings of representatives of different community groups such as the school board, YMCA, church groups, Capilano College, and others who were concerned about lack of counselling facilities for young people in the community. "Certainly, the schools have their counsellors, but they have heavy loads to carry and often the best counselling environment isn't an office in a school," says Hollick-Kenyon. "This service is designed to act as a supplementary career counselling resource to secondary school counsellors. It will reach out to young people in the areas where they congregrate, and deal only with their areas of concern.

"The service will provide information to assist students in selecting career goals. This information will include job opportunities, forecasted manpower needs, and availability of higher education."

Hollick-Kenyon says another important area of counselling will be providing help for students who have medical or emotional problems.

"If necessary, we will make direct contact, through a radio-telephone in the van, with doctors, or social workers, or others in a position to help, and arrange an appointment on the spot."

The van, which is being provided courtesy of Capilano Volkswagen Ltd., will be on the road before the end of May. It will be staffed by Bob Bagshaw, a graduate student in counselling at the University of B.C.

"Mr. Bagshaw has had wide experience as regional director for Eastern Canada of the Young Life movement. He has worked ex-

Bob Bagshaw holds informal discussions with students at Ambleside Park.

Continued on Back Page

When this newsletter appeared in 1971, Capilano College had not yet moved to its new location in the District of North Vancouver. Today the college is a university with a student population of 7,500. NVMA 1971-25

An advertisement for the grand opening of Capilano Mall in 1975. The mall was located in a low-lying area of Marine Drive once known as "Skunk Hollow." NVMA 1975-23

Top: Canadian Park and Tilford Distilleries opened a public garden on its property in 1969. The distillery is gone, replaced by a shopping mall and film studio, but the garden remains. NVMA 1172-24

Bottom: This is what Park and Tilford looked like as a distillery, before it was redeveloped as a mall in the 1980s. NVMA 9275

North Vancouver, where construction got underway in 1970. When it opened in 1973, Capilano College had a student population of 1,965. Over the years, more buildings were added, and in 1990, the college offered its first four-year bachelor degree. Since 2008, Capilano has been an accredited university.

Capilano University is known for its School of Motion Picture Arts, so it is appropriate that North Vancouver has become a major film production centre. The story begins with, of all things, a distillery. In 1957, Canadian Park and Tilford Distilleries opened an operation on a 24-acre (9.7-ha) site west of the north end of the Second Narrows Bridge. A few years later the company took an unused corner of the property and transformed it into a public garden as a gift to the community. Park and Tilford Gardens officially opened in January 1969 and has been a feature attraction ever since. When the distillery closed in 1983, its then-owner, Schenley Canada, planned to sell the entire site for redevelopment. After much controversy, the gardens were saved, while the rest of the property became a shopping centre and, to the north, a film studio: North Shore Studios, built by Hollywood producer Stephen J. Cannell. Cannell had already been filming his hit television series *21 Jump Street*, featuring a young Johnny Depp, at Carson Graham Secondary. *Jump Street*, which debuted in 1987, was one of the first major television shows to film on location in the Lower Mainland.

North Shore Studios continued its production of hit television series with the enormously successful science fiction

A publicity poster for the classic film *McCabe and Mrs. Miller*. The photograph on the poster was taken by North Vancouver photographer Eric Hayes and shows some of the sets built by North Shore squatters from Maplewood.
NVMA Item 1970-19

The Lynn Valley library. Today's modern facilities have come a long way from the District's first purpose-built library, an unheated shack on Edgemont Boulevard that opened at the beginning of 1953. Scott Robarts photo

conspiracy thriller *The X-Files*. Filmed largely at the studios and at locations around the Lower Mainland, it began airing in 1993 and its first five seasons were made on the North Shore before production moved to Los Angeles. North Shore Studios was purchased and renamed "Lionsgate Studios" in 1997, but returned to its original name in 2006 when property developer Nat Bosa bought it. Other locations around North Vancouver have featured in a variety of television series and motion pictures. Highlights include the escape drama *The Fugitive*, partly shot at Cleveland Dam; the mystery *Double Jeopardy*, starring Tommy Lee Jones and Ashley Judd, with scenes shot in Edgemont Village; and the long-running sci-fi television series *Stargate SG-1*. Not forgetting one of the earliest films shot on the North Shore, Robert Altman's classic hippie western, *McCabe & Mrs. Miller*, featuring Warren Beatty and Julie Christie and released in 1971. The film was shot in West Vancouver and Squamish, but many of the sets were built by residents of the squatter community at Maplewood. In a sense, *McCabe* was North Vancouver's initiation into the film industry.

Looking to the Future

The District of North Vancouver is a sprawling municipality covering a lot of territory, which makes it a challenge for local government to provide services to such a dispersed population; this was one reason the City and District separated in the first place. In response to this challenge, the District has adopted a "network of centres" model for future development. This model attempts to manage growth by creating concentrations of residential and commercial development linked by efficient transportation corridors. According to the Official Community Plan (OCP) adopted in 2011, the District will feature eight distinct neighbourhoods (along with the First Nations reserves). Two will be so-called "Town Centres" (Lynn Valley and Lynn Creek), while the remaining six will be "Village Centres" (Lions Gate, Edgemont, Queensdale, Maplewood, Parkgate and Deep Cove). The Town Centres will be transportation hubs containing significant commercial enterprises and major public facilities such as libraries and community centres. Village centres will provide a focus for a surrounding neighbourhood, with local shopping and a more intimate "urban village" atmosphere. By focusing as much as 90 percent of future development in these compact "centres," planners hope to improve transportation, reduce the community's environmental footprint and make it more economical to provide public services.

Another challenge facing the District is the "graying" of its population. A quarter of all residents are now over fifty-five years of age. At the same time, the percentage of young adults has declined, as has the number of jobs available locally, raising questions about the economic future of the community. (Another indicator is the decline in the number of school-age children, resulting in the closure of several schools.) If there isn't a healthy number of jobs available locally, it means that residents must commute to work, with the environmental downside that implies.

Seventy percent of housing in the District is in the form of detached homes, which has implications for transportation, efficiency of public services and ecological footprint. As part of its OCP, the District is encouraging a wider variety of housing types in the hopes of providing affordable housing opportunities for lower-income residents.

By contrast, the focus of commercial and residential development in North Vancouver City is in Lower and Central Lonsdale Avenue and along the Marine Drive corridor. At the moment, Central and Lower Lonsdale contain a little more than 60 percent of the City's population, and a majority of new immigrants to the community are choosing to live there.

Like the District, the City plans to focus future development in high-density urban areas and along transportation corridors in order to reap the benefits that densification produces.

If managing growth is one of the challenges facing local governments on the North Shore, preserving the natural environment is another. From the beginning of the District in 1891, people have been attracted to North Vancouver because it is the gateway to the local mountains and the recreational opportunities they provide. Few other communities are so defined by their natural setting.

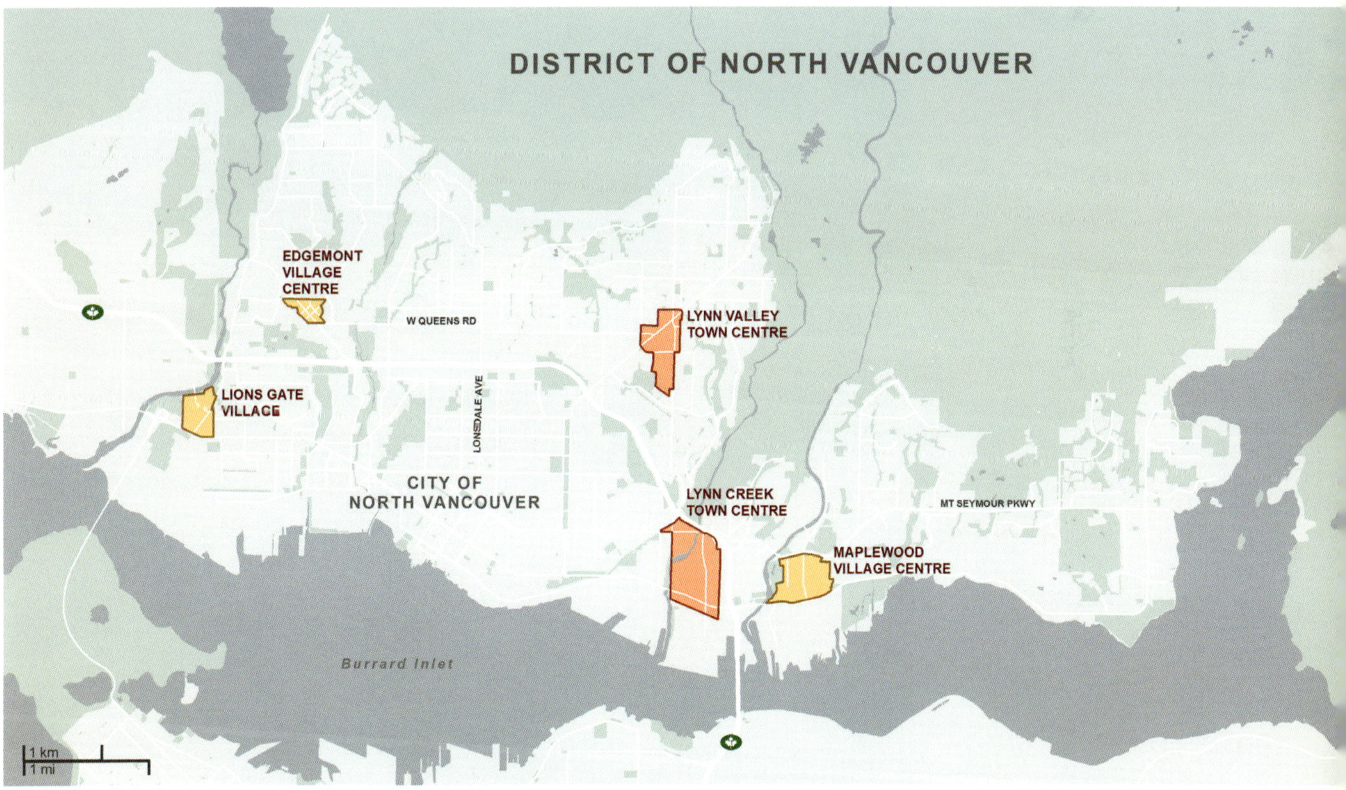

This map shows the village and town centres where the District intends to focus growth in the future.

ON NATURE'S EDGE

North Vancouver enjoys a spectacular natural setting. Though it is a modern urban community located just minutes from downtown Vancouver, its closeness to the mountain wilderness gives the North Shore a unique identity. From the beginning it has been a mecca for outdoor enthusiasts, whether kayakers, canoeists, mountain bikers, hikers, skiers or snowboarders. The preservation of this rich legacy of wilderness and parks has played an important part in the community's history.

Long before newcomers ventured into the backcountry, the First Nations were at home on the slopes of the North Shore Mountains. The Squamish and Tsleil-Waututh people mainly lived in villages and campsites along the shores of Burrard Inlet, but they accessed the back country using a network of trails. There, they hunted large animals such as elk, bear, mountain goat and deer, pursued spiritual practices, gathered many different kinds of plants for subsistence and medicines, and found wood, stone and bark to manufacture tools, clothing and other implements. Dugout canoes were fashioned from cedar logs, hollowed out and shaped with stone tools. Many of the ancient campsites are now protected by provincial archaeological legislation.

Above: A map from the "Progress '66" special edition of the Citizen newspaper in 1966 features the recreational possibilities of the North Shore. NVMA Pamphlet 1966–15

Preceding pages: Three young women bathing at a secluded beach on the North Shore, ca. 1910. NVMA 4019

West Vancouver photographer Claire Downing snaps a picture of himself posing on a stump in the middle of a cut on Grouse Mountain, ca. 1901.
VPL 4824

The First Nations were skilled climbers and mountaineers. When Euro-Canadians approached the mountains for the first time, they required the help of guides from the First Nations' communities. Two of the prominent peaks on the North Shore are the snow-capped Lions looking south across Burrard Inlet to Vancouver and beyond. The Squamish people know them as "The Two Sisters," embodying the daughters of a great chief whose coming-of-age potlatch brought peace to the warring tribes of the coast. One of the peaks was scaled by settlers for the first time in 1889, when Su-a pu-luck (Joe Capilano) led a group of non-Aboriginal hunters into the mountains in pursuit of mountain goats, and they ended up at the top of West Lion.

As Vancouver grew, residents looked across the Inlet and were attracted by the beauty and challenge of the mountains. The North Shore brought wilderness right to the edge of the city. The three major peaks —Seymour, Grouse and Hollyburn—and the surrounding slopes were a promise and an opportunity. They provided clean

Top left: A detail of an advertisement for the original Grouse Mountain Chalet, which was destroyed by fire in 1962. NVMA 1924-4

Above: The original Grouse Mountain Chalet opened at the summit of the mountain in the mid-1920s. It was possible to drive to the chalet, which featured a fine restaurant, a ballroom and rooms for $3.50 to $4.50 a night. NVMA 417

Spectacular views of the Lower Mainland were what attracted hikers and mountaineers to the North Shore Mountains. The photo shows the Lions Gate Bridge crossing into Stanley Park; Vancouver Island is faintly visible on the horizon. NVMA BB.157

North Vancouver–born architect Bob Booth, an avid mountaineer, on a hike behind Grouse Mountain in the 1940s. NVMA BB117

This iconic photograph of the Lions with Don and Phyllis Munday in the foreground dates to 1920. NVMA 5681

Four men at the cabin owned by William John Trythall near the top of Mosquito Creek on the slopes of Grouse Mountain, ca. 1908. CVA AM54-S4-Mount P74

drinking water for the metropolis, and a chance to venture into the "back of beyond" to experience wild nature within a few kilometres of home.

In the early days, the mountains were accessible, but it took a real effort to get to them. Hikers, and later skiers, had to hoist their backpacks and trek up into the backcountry from the waterfront. The waterworks road that opened alongside the Capilano River in the late 1880s (now Capilano Road) improved access, as did the streetcars that travelled north to the top of Lonsdale and west from the ferry landing to Capilano Road by the end of 1911. Still, it took most of a day to reach the mountains. According to local historian Roy Pallant, the first mountain cabin on the North Shore belonged to Vancouver printer William John Trythall, who built it in 1892 on property he owned near the top of Mosquito Creek (originally called "Trythall Creek"). Trythall left the cabin open for climbers to rest, replenish their water supply, and stay overnight if necessary.

"Grouse Mountain in those days [1920s] was considered to be quite a hike. We used to pay a nickel on the streetcar to go downtown, a nickel a ride on the ferry and a nickel on the old Lonsdale car. That would take you to the top of Lonsdale, and from then on we hiked up the old road . . . crossed Mosquito Creek and went up the old Grouse Mountain Trail which was pretty rugged with fallen timber. In those days, Grouse Mountain was really a beautiful hike."

—Art Cooper, pioneer mountaineer

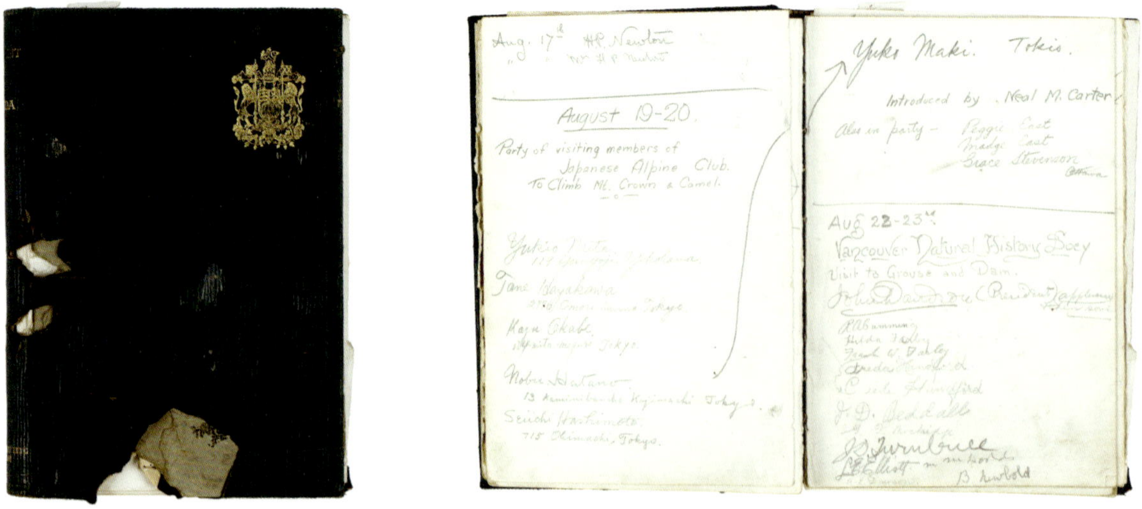

A bear broke into the BC Mountaineering Club cabin on Grouse Mountain and left this claw print in the club journal as a calling card. NVMA BCMC fonds 205 Shawn McDonald photo

In 1907 a group of Vancouver climbers formed the Vancouver Mountaineering Club (two years later it became the BC Mountaineering Club). Members of the club blazed trails, shared maps, made the first ascent of several local mountains and built a small shack on the lower slope of Grouse Mountain as an informal headquarters for their activities. Three years later they replaced this so-called "Red Shack" with a more substantial log cabin higher up the mountain, where members based themselves while they trekked the surrounding backcountry. For a time, Dickson Kells's Capilano Hotel, with its Swiss chalet ambience, bar and dining room, was the club's informal headquarters. The North Shore Mountains had an almost spiritual attraction in these early days. "The spell of the great out-of-doors is upon you," wrote one hiking enthusiast in *British Columbia Magazine* in 1911, "and you realize the joy of living that you have never known before."

A group of hikers on the Mosquito Creek trail in the early 1900s. Note that hikers were expected to dress appropriately, which meant long skirts for the women, ties for the men. NVMA 10082

The club prided itself on drawing members from all walks of life and all levels of income. The main requirement for membership was a dedication to mountaineering. BCMC members were

Members of the BC Mountaineering Club pause for a cup of warmth while snowshoeing on Grouse Mountain in 1921. Phyllis Munday is third from left; Don Munday extreme right. NVMA 5682

Right: The cover from a BC Electric Railway company map promoting hiking trails on the North Shore, 1934. NVMA 1934-2

Far right: Waxing skis at one of the Grouse Mountian cabins. NVMA DS.115

Stella Davidson (l.) with a friend at her cabin, Ski-Larks, on Grouse Mountain. Stella met her husband, Bill Simpson, on Grouse and the couple helped to build several log cabins for friends. NVMA DS.040

the first non-Aboriginal climbers to summit many of the mountains on the North Shore, and they hacked out many kilometres of trails. The first trail guide, produced by members, appeared in the 1960s, published by the *Vancouver Province* newspaper. In 1973 a more extensive guide was produced, *103 Hikes in Southwestern British Columbia*. Revised over the years, it has sold more than one hundred thousand copies. From its beginning, the BCMC has been active in the movement to create provincial parks and preserve the mountain wilderness.

Between the wars, the Grouse Mountain Ski Club formed for those who preferred to get their exercise schussing down the slopes. Access to Grouse improved in the mid-1920s when Vancouver entrepreneur William Curtis Shelly built a paved toll road up the mountain, an extension of today's Mountain Highway, and a log chalet at the summit. Aside from owning a variety of businesses in the city, Shelly was prominent in local politics, serving on Vancouver City Council and the Parks Board and was even a one-term member of the provincial legislature, where he served as finance minister. Shelly's mountain getaway was an impressive building, constructed by Scandinavian craftsmen without using a nail. It featured a large stone fireplace, bearskin rugs and carved handrails on all the staircases. For a time it was very popular; one journalist described a trail of limousines driving up the highway on a typical Saturday evening. But then the Depression arrived, business fell off, and, like so many properties on the North Shore, in 1935 the chalet reverted to the

Above right: This decal advertising the Chalet dates from the middle of the Depression when business was foundering. The road to the summit was an extension of Mountain Highway; it still exists but is no longer open to the public. NVMA 1935-6

Above: An ice axe was part of the basic equipment for an early mountaineer. The wooden-handled axe doubled as a walking stick. The steel head was double-ended: one end was sharply pointed for helping to climb up a steep slope of snow or ice; the other end was shaped more like an adze for cutting steps. NVMA 2011.86 Shawn McDonald photo

Ski clubs flourished on the North Shore Mountains during the 1930s. NVMA DS.142

District for non-payment of taxes. It was sold to private investors after World War II, among them the Cromie family, who also owned the *Vancouver Sun* newspaper. The *Sun* offered free ski lessons to subscribers and the chalet, until it burned down in 1962, was a favourite destination for Vancouverites on summer evenings when they danced to the piano stylings of Hugo Sartorello. In the mid-1950s the Grouse Mountain Ski Club merged with another club, the Tyee Ski Runners, and today the Grouse Mountain Tyee Ski Club continues to sponsor races and conduct lessons for dedicated young skiers.

Ski jumping used to enjoy huge popularity on the North Shore, especially among immigrants from Scandinavia. During the 1920s the first jumps were built on Grouse, Hollyburn and Seymour mountains, and during the subsequent decades, competitions attracted crowds of enthusiastic onlookers. The local mountains produced some of the finest jumpers in Canada until the mid-1960s when interest in ski jumping petered out on the North Shore. Given the expense of building and maintaining jumps and the logistics of organizing competitions, most people preferred the simpler pleasures of downhill skiing.

In 1949 Canada's first double chairlift—billed as the "Chairway to the Stars"—began carrying hikers and skiers up to the top of Grouse, and the opening of the lift revitalized skiing on the mountain. In 1965 a new owner, Grouse Mountain Resorts, under the leadership of Vancouver businessman Andrew Saxton, took control with ambitious plans for expansion. At the beginning of 1966 the Skyride aerial

The Skyride gondola opened in 1966, carrying visitors to the top of Grouse Mountain. NVMA 15984

The Grouse Mountain double chairlift opened in 1949, revitalizing skiing on the mountain. NVMA 8466

tramway began operations carrying visitors from the top of Capilano Road up the mountain to the chalet where a new restaurant opened that summer. (The larger Super Skyride replaced the original in 1976.) Since 1974 the mountain has been owned by the McLaughlin family who have been responsible for adding a range of attractions, including a zipline, a movie theatre and a wildlife refuge. Today Grouse Mountain is one of the most popular destinations in the Lower Mainland for day skiers and snowboarders. During the 2010 Winter Olympics, the American television network NBC located its broadcast centre at the top of the mountain. And let's not forget the hikers. The Grouse Grind is a steep, 3-kilometre trail up the face of the mountain, nicknamed "Mother Nature's Stairmaster." It was built in the early 1980s as a conditioning trail for serious hikers, but it has been rebuilt and improved since that time and is now used by more than 150,000 fitness buffs annually.

Seymour Mountain, because it was a bit more remote, was slower to develop as a ski area. Members of the BC Mountaineering Club made the first official climb to the summit in 1908 but it was not until the 1930s that skiers began visiting the slopes in any numbers. With the opening of the Dollarton Highway in 1931 the mountain became slightly more accessible, and in 1936, the province created Mount Seymour Provincial Park and leased operations of the ski hills to a private operator, Harold Enquist, who built the first ski lodge and the first rope tow on the

A DAY ON THE MOUNTAIN

"A party of school children under the leadership of [Walter] Draycott made a successful ascent to Grouse Mountain via the scenic highway on Good Friday last. The start of the trip was made from the rendezvous, Lynn Valley Post Office, at 8:15 a.m., thence up Centre Road [Mountain Highway] to the Highway. A wide road, capable of accommodating two touring cars abreast with plenty of space between, was easy travelling for a distance of approximately five miles. Much courtesy was shown by the workmen as blasting operations were being carried on . . . Snow was encountered about the 3,000 foot contour line. With childish delight they entered into winter sports among the snow. As the party reached the source of Mosquito Creek a snow-storm added to the picturesque wintery scene . . . The site of the proposed hotel of eight acres was reached by two p.m. Huge logs are being hauled in by a donkey engine for the building of the hotel. Don Munday's cabin was the final objective, where the whole party were introduced to little Edith Munday, who with keen delight showed them her little snowshoes. . . . The return trip was made by the trail to Lonsdale Avenue. Before nightfall the party were back in their homes, having keenly enjoyed the expedition, which is the first of its kind up the new Highway."

—*North Shore Press,* April 9, 1926

mountain. With the construction of road access in 1942, Mount Seymour joined Grouse and Hollyburn as popular North Shore ski and hiking destinations. Along with day visitors, there were as many as three hundred cabins spread along the side of the mountain by the 1950s, most of which have since disappeared. "Cabin culture," as it was known, was characterized by resourcefulness, self-reliance, and camaraderie. Cabin dwellers were a long way from "civilization" and had to rely on themselves and their neighbours if anything went wrong. When they weren't out hiking and skiing, they got together for work parties, dinners and informal dances. Among the regular visitors to the mountain were members of the UBC's Varsity Outdoor Club (VOC). This student-run club built its first cabin on Grouse Mountain in 1929, then relocated to a larger cabin on Seymour in 1951. This cabin remained the centre of VOC activities until the mid-1960s when the club again moved its headquarters, this time to Whistler. The provincial government retained ownership of the lodge and the lifts until 1984 when operations on the mountain were privatized.

Local mountains offer a far wider variety of activities today than they once did. With the advent of climate change, winters appear to be getting shorter and warmer, not good news for local skiers. In response, the mountains have become year-round destinations offering nature-based experiences for all seasons. Mountain biking and ziplining are just two activities, not to mention snowboarding, tubing and snowshoeing, which have joined skiing as popular winter sports.

Phyllis and Don Munday on the summit of Mount Victoria in the Canadian Rockies, 1925. The Mundays, legendary climbers, scaled most of the tallest peaks in British Columbia. NVMA 5650

FIRST LADY OF THE MOUNTAINS

Phyllis Munday arrived in Vancouver with her family when she was a young girl and climbed her first mountain, Grouse, when she was just ten years old. She married Don Munday in 1920, and together, they climbed many of the province's highest peaks and were among the pioneer climbers who explored the Coast Mountains for the first time. Phyllis was also the founder of the Girl Guide movement in BC. As she told an interviewer:

> I used to go up Grouse Mountain on my own, or with a few Girl Guides. We started off from home with a skirt on. You were never seen on the street with a bloomer or a pair of pants or anything like that. It just wasn't done in those days. So we'd wear our skirts on the streetcar from home, and the ferry, and the streetcar in North Van, and then up to the trail and cache our skirts under a log. That meant, of course, you always had to come back the same way to get your skirt, because otherwise you couldn't go home.[36]

Phyllis Munday was awarded the Order of Canada in 1973.

Above: Phyllis Munday, with her daughter Edith, set to go hiking with an ice axe and a 26-kilogram pack, ca. 1923.
NVMA 5652

Below: In 1998 Canada Post issued this 45-cent stamp commemorating Phyllis Munday. She was the first woman to reach the top of Mount Robson, the highest peak in the Canadian Rockies.
NVMA 1998-9

NORTH SHORE RESCUE

Parks and outdoor recreation are at the heart of the North Vancouver experience. The great outdoors are what draw so many people to the community, both to live and to visit. Perhaps nobody better represents this link between community and wilderness than the volunteers who risk their own lives to track down wayward hikers, snowboarders and skiers who have gotten into trouble on the mountains.

In the fall of 1956 three hikers got lost on Mount Seymour in very bad weather. After six days, search parties located one of the missing men and the Royal Canadian Air Force (RCAF) search and rescue team helicoptered him to safety. A second member of the missing party managed to find his own way off the mountain, but tragically, the third man died from exposure. In response to this incident, members of the BC Mountaineering Club organized the Mountain Rescue Group (MRG), volunteers on call to assist the RCAF and the RCMP in rescue work.

A search and rescue team looks for missing hikers on Mount Seymour in 1956. This operation, only partly successful, led to the creation of the first volunteer mountain rescue group, forerunner to North Shore Rescue. NVMA 10341

During the 1960s the work of the MRG was taken up by another volunteer search and rescue team, North Shore Rescue (NSR). This group was founded in 1965 in the middle of the Cold War as a civil defence team, but experience showed that there was a greater need for rescue operations in the wilderness than preparing for a nuclear attack that never came. Members of NSR undergo hours of training and regularly endanger their own lives to track down people who have lost their way on the mountains. Thousands of climbers, hikers, boarders, snowshoers and skiers have benefited from the skills of the volunteers. With the growing popularity of the North Shore Mountains as an outdoor recreation area has come a growing need for the emergency services of NSR.

North Shore Rescue volunteers engaged in a variety of rescue operations. North Shore Rescue photos

Phyllis Munday, climbing beneath Mount Goodsir in the Rocky Mountains in Yoho National Park. NVMA 9783

NAMING THE NORTH SHORE MOUNTAINS

Grouse Mountain was named by the first recorded hikers to attain its summit. That was in 1894. Bushwhacking their way up the snow-covered slope, the hikers spotted and shot a blue grouse, a game bird native to the area. They commemorated the occasion by naming the mountain after their victim.

Mount Seymour is named for Frederick Seymour, a governor of British Columbia before the colony became a province of Canada. He was not a very effectual leader—historian Margaret Ormsby called him BC's "forgotten governor"—but the local mountain nonetheless recalls his name.

Hollyburn was the name of the waterfront home owned by West Vancouver pioneer John Lawson. He had planted holly trees on the property, and in 1912, the well-known botanist John Davidson named the mountain area while surveying the plant life.

Other local peaks include Goat Mountain, named for the mountain goats that used to be plentiful in the area; Mount Fromme, named for the pioneer mill owner in Lynn Valley; Crown Mountain, named for its shape; and Mount Strachan, named for a British naval commander.

District Parks

George Grant Mackay, the Scottish engineer and developer who built the first suspension bridge across the Capilano River. CVA Port P201

Within the District proper, about 13 percent of its 160.5 square kilometre land area is managed parkland. One of the oldest of these parks encompasses much of the lower valley of the Capilano River. Capilano River Regional Park originated with a Scotsman named George Grant Mackay, who only lived in the Vancouver area for five years but left an indelible mark. Mackay arrived in 1888 at the age of sixty-six and set to work acquiring property. Along with a house in Vancouver's West End, he purchased several thousand hectares of land in the Capilano Valley and built a second home overlooking the river at what was known as "First Canyon." He wrote to a friend back home, "It is a magnificent country and far exceeds my expectations

Outdoors enthusiasts of all ages take advantage of the District's proximity to parks and wilderness. NVMA photo

in every way. I am very glad I came out."[37] Mackay built the first suspension bridge across the river. With the help of young August Jack Khatsahlano, later a revered Squamish elder, Mackay constructed the bridge out of rope and cedar planks and had a team of horses swim one end across the river. (On a larger scale, Mackay is also credited with originating the idea of a bridge across the First Narrows.) Mackay's bridge, which was replaced by a wire cable crossing in 1903, became a popular destination for hikers.

In 1907, as the BC Electric Railway Company planned for the extension of its streetcar line west to the Capilano (not opened until May 1911), it purchased 160 acres of land along the river north of the suspension bridge, extending as far as today's Cleveland Dam. At the time not many people lived in the area and the company decided to develop a park as a destination for riders on the streetcar. The BCER did much to promote hiking in the mountains, producing brochures and maps that illustrated the popular trails and how the streetcar could be used to access them. In 1924 the BCER donated its land on the

WILD RIDERS

Mountain biking got its start in Marin County, California, during the 1970s, but it was not long afterwards that a handful of daredevil trail riders pioneered the sport on the North Shore. The centre of the action was Deep Cove and the Cove Bike Shop, opened in 1981 by Chaz Romalis and a couple of friends. They imported the earliest fat-tired bikes from California and began building trails up in the mountains behind the Cove. Soon they were fashioning their own frames, adapted to conditions on the North Shore, and the sport took off, making North Vancouver the centre of trail riding in Canada and one of the hot spots in North America.

By the 1990s mountain bikers had acquired a reputation for recklessness and operating outside the law. They were building trails on public property and making stunt structures that threatened injury to less skilled riders. Some residents wanted to close the trails to bikers, or at least charge fees to use them (despite the fact that many of the trails had been built by the bikers themselves). In 1997 a group of local riders formed the North Shore Mountain Bike Association to act as a voice for the bikers. The Association advocated for open access, built and maintained trails and worked to improve the renegade image of the bikers. Today mountain biking is as popular as ever on the North Shore, enjoyed by a wide range of age groups and abilities.

The difficult mountain terrain poses an attractive challenge to mountain bikers on the North Shore. Todd Fiander photo

Capilano to the Vancouver Board of Trade, and it eventually became the regional park we know today. One of its features is a salmon hatchery, opened in 1971 to replenish salmon stocks in the river that had been reduced by the construction of the Cleveland Dam.

Back to George Mackay's suspension bridge. It came into the hands of Edward Mahon, one of the early land developers involved in the creation of the municipality of North Vancouver. Mahon built a teahouse and made other improvements to the property. Subsequent owners added to the attraction until, in 1953, Rae Mitchell purchased the site. Mitchell rebuilt the bridge, developed trails and opened a gift shop. Today the Capilano Suspension Bridge, which hangs 70 metres above the river, is owned by Mitchell's daughter Nancy Stibbard and is one of the most popular attractions in the entire province, attracting about 800,000 visitors a year.

The North Shore is marked by many rivers and streams flowing down its steep slopes to the inlet. Some of the larger ones have trails and narrow parks following their winding course. Mosquito Creek is a case

Mountain bikers construct their own ladders, bridges and stunt structures to navigate the steep slopes of the North Shore Mountains. Todd Fiander photo

in point. The creek originates high up on the slopes of Grouse Mountain and tumbles its way through the District and the City before emptying into the inlet in the Mission Reserve at the bottom of Bewicke Avenue. Like most North Shore streams, the creek was logged extensively in its upper reaches in the late nineteenth century, while its estuary was filled in for industrial developments from before World War I (the "Fell Fill" site). During World War II the federal government built about four hundred single-family bungalows along the lower reaches of the creek to accommodate workers in the shipyards. After the war these homes were replaced by more modern residences and by commercial development, and the mid-reaches of the creek opened to residential development.

A colour postcard shows the Lynn Canyon suspension bridge shortly after it opened in 1912. NVMA 5202

The rock pools of Lynn Canyon have attracted generations of swimmers to the park on hot summer days. NVMA 11174

In 1966 it was suggested that the name "mosquito" did not send a benign message to people who might use the creek and its trails, and part of the adjoining parkland was renamed "William Griffin Park" after a local councillor, though the creek retained its original name. Not surprisingly, extensive changes to the watershed due to logging, flood control and urbanization made it unfit for the salmon and trout that used to inhabit the creek. Since the mid-1990s, however, work has been done to restore habitat and open fish access once again. The cycle of destruction and rehabilitation is typical of the recent history of many of the smaller streams that criss-cross the North Shore.

At the same time, some of the larger rivers became the focus of more ambitious park development. Aside from the Capilano, another example is Lynn Canyon Park. The original land was donated to the District by the twin brothers Donald and A. D. McTavish, a pair of Vancouver businessmen who were also enthusiastic mountaineers. The District contributed another 10 acres along the canyon, and when the BC Electric Railway extended its streetcar line up Lynn Valley Road to the entrance, the municipal park opened in 1912. One of its biggest boosters was District councillor J. P. Crawford, whose idea it was to build the suspension bridge across the canyon. That same year, local residents put on the first Lynn Valley Day, a community celebration that has been held annually ever since. The bridge remains a focus of the park, as does the Ecology Centre added in 1971, an education facility providing programs and displays about natural history, the environment and sustainability issues.

North up Lynn Creek from the canyon is another, more rugged green space: Lynn Headwaters Regional Park. Much of this park encompasses land worked over by the early loggers, and evidence of their activities can be seen in the notched stumps and the occasional piece of rusted machinery. The park has trails suited to the casual walker and also features challenging backcountry hiking through steep, mountainous terrain. At 4,685 hectares, Lynn Headwaters is the largest park managed by Metro Vancouver. Lynn Creek supplied drinking water to the City of North Vancouver from the 1920s until 1983, and as a result the watershed was closed to the public. When flooding damaged the water intakes and the City joined the Greater Vancouver Water District, the Headwaters area became publicly accessible.

On the lower slopes of Mount Seymour to the east of Lynn Creek is the Lower Seymour Conservation Reserve, known popularly as the "Seymour Demonstration Forest." At one time, the valley of the Seymour River was thought to be a potential route linking Burrard Inlet with the interior of the province. In 1875 work began on a packhorse trail running alongside the river through the mountains toward Squamish and Pemberton. The plan was to drive cattle down from the Interior to feed meat-hungry communities in the Lower Mainland and construction crews building the Canadian Pacific Railway. Known as the "Lillooet Trail," it terminated at sea level near the foot of what is now Lillooet Road. It was completed

LITTLE HOUSE IN THE FOREST

Near the entrance to Lynn Headwaters Regional Park sits a small blue house that is more than one hundred years old. The BC Mills House was originally located in Lower Lonsdale in the City of North Vancouver, where it was erected by its owner Henry Pybus in 1908. Pybus was a sea captain who commanded three of the CP's famous "Empress" trans-Pacific steamships. The building is called the "BC Mills House" because it was one of the houses mass-produced between 1904 and 1910 by the BC Mills Timber and Trading Company, otherwise known as "Hastings Mill," at one time Vancouver's largest employer. Henry Pybus, like any other customer of BC Mills, simply ordered the house from a catalogue and received it in pieces in a kit. The pieces were numbered and came with a set of instructions so that even the least competent owners would have no trouble assembling their new homes. The company was appealing especially to the settlers who were flooding into the Canadian West before World War I and needed inexpensive housing that was easy to construct.

After years of neglect, the derelict Pybus house was going to be torn down. But long-time City councillor Stella Jo Dean saw the historic importance of the dwelling, the first prefab house on the North Shore. Thanks to her initiative, the house was rescued, restored by volunteers and moved to Lynn Headwaters in 1998, where it became a small museum featuring information about the logging history of Lynn Valley.

The BC Mills House, abandoned and neglected on its original site before it was moved to Lynn Headwaters Park and refurbished as a small museum.
NVMA 1172-19

Horse and buggy on the Lillooet Trail, ca. 1915. When the trail was completed in 1877 it proved too challenging to drive cattle along and fell into disuse. NVMA 8402

in 1877, though it proved impractical to maintain and was seldom used for its intended purpose. But it did open the lower Seymour to outsiders, and during the 1880s and 1890s, much of the land in the valley was pre-empted, mainly by loggers. Though Vancouver obtained its water from the Capilano River, city officials sought a second source, and in 1908, several municipalities, including North Vancouver, began drawing water from the Seymour. In order to protect the source, the province set aside all the land in the watershed that had not already been alienated.

During the 1920s logging interests fought a spirited battle to allow forestry within the North Shore watersheds, but with the creation in the mid-1920s of the Greater Vancouver Water District, all the private land in the upper Seymour was gradually bought up, and by 1936, logging in the watershed area had been phased out. Today the Seymour reservoir provides about a third of Metro Vancouver's drinking water and remains off-limits to the public. Below the dam, however, is a 5,668-ha area with more than 100 kilometres of trails. Created in 1987, the Demonstration Forest made the Lower Seymour area accessible to the public for the first time in sixty years. The main feature is a paved trailway leading 10 kilometres north, as far as the dam. It is a popular attraction for cyclists and inline skaters as well as hikers.

At least one park has been developed in collaboration with the First Nations. Whey-ah-Wichen (Cates Park) is a 22.3-ha park located at Roche Point, at the extreme eastern end of the District. It was developed jointly by the District and the Tsleil-Waututh Nation and is the largest waterfront park in the District. The park is in the traditional territory of the Tsleil-Waututh, and archaeological evidence suggests that the area has been used for at least 3,500 years. Before World War II

LOCAL BRAND MAKES GOOD

Given North Vancouver's location at the base of the mountains, it should be no surprise that one of the leading manufacturers of outdoor equipment is located in the community.

In 1989 two young climbers, Dave Lane and Jeremy Guard, started making climbing equipment out of Lane's North Shore home. Calling themselves "Rock Solid Manufacturing," they relied on their own experience in the backcountry to manufacture high-quality gear.

In 1991 the operation's name changed to "Arc'teryx" (after *Archaeopteryx lithographica*, the earliest known bird) and the company began introducing a series of innovative products to the market, including climbing harnesses, backpacks and a range of outerwear for climbers, skiers and snowboarders.

Today Arc'teryx is a division of Amer Sports, a sporting goods company based in Finland, but its headquarters remain in North Vancouver.

The dairy farm at Maplewood in the 1940s, owned by Jack and Helen Smyth. NVMA 15424

the Roche Point neighbourhood was home to extensive sawmill operations, and a significant community of millworkers and their families was augmented by fishermen and holiday cottagers. In 1931 the completion of the Dollarton Highway allowed improved access by automobile, and following the war, the area attracted new industries and new residents.

J. H. Cates, son of the founder of the towboat company Cates Towing (now part of Seaspan) as well as a prominent provincial politician, had purchased land at Roche Point as a possible site to relocate the family business, but these plans had not developed. In 1950 the District purchased this land from the Cates family and dedicated it as "Cates Park." At this time the park was occupied by a small community of squatter's shacks. Most of these residents were gone by 1958, their shacks demolished. The District purchased the remaining property that now constitutes the park during the 1990s. Over the years, Cates Park has been the location of a variety of community celebrations, from potlatches and Tsleil-Waututh canoe races, to Lions Club events, to hippie "be-ins" during the 1970s, to an annual arts festival (between 1990 and 2010)

Dozens of volunteers turned out on a special day in 1905 to begin clearing the land to make way for the creation of Victoria Park, the first component in the "Green Necklace" of boulevards, parks and greenways. NVMA 53

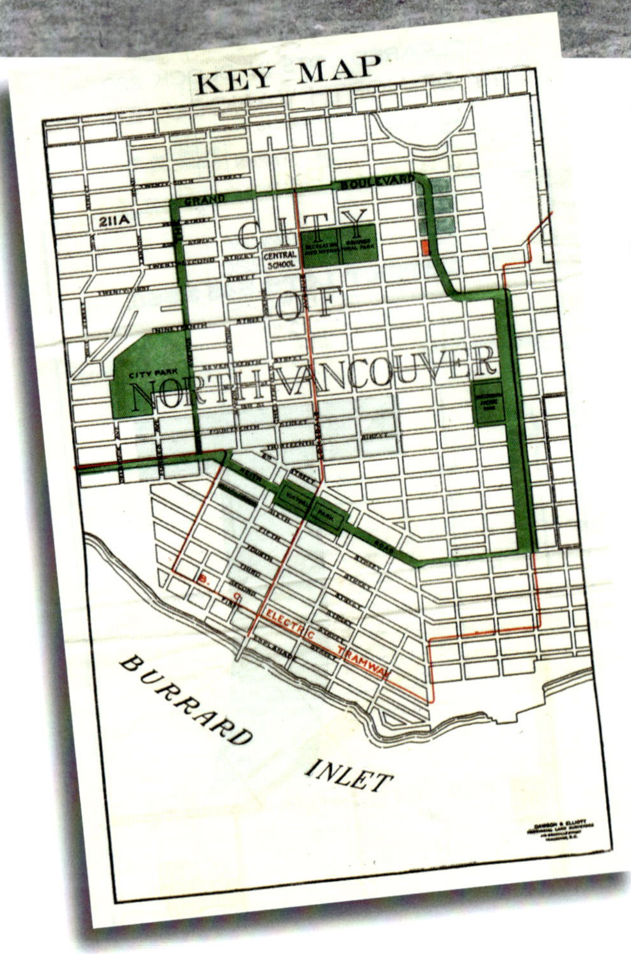

Above: Victoria Park, shown here in the 1920s, has been an important green space in North Vancouver for more than a century. NVMA 11410

Left: This map shows the Green Necklace of interconnected greenways as it was originally conceived. The concept dates back to the early days of the community and is coming to completion more than a century later. NVMA Item 863

called "Under the Volcano" in honour of Malcolm Lowry, the most prominent of the bohemian squatters. In 2001 the Tsleil-Waututh and the District government signed an agreement formalizing their co-management of the park.

A unique park experience is offered by Maplewood Farm, east of the Seymour River. In the early 1900s North Vancouver was a very rural community, marked by many farms producing dairy products, fruit and vegetables. Maplewood is the last remaining farm from this era. For many years a functioning dairy operation, it produced milk that was delivered to homes throughout the District. In 1970 the property was taken over by the District government and converted to a "children's farm," which opened in 1975. The 2-hectare site exposes youngsters to farm animals and the North Shore's rural heritage. Just to the east of the farm along the waterfront is the Maplewood Conservation Area, a 35-hectare wetland of unique interest to birdwatchers. The conservation area, which is on land donated by the Port of Vancouver and the District, includes trails and salt marshes and is managed by the Wild Bird Trust, providing protected habitat for scores of bird species. With so much of the North Vancouver waterfront built over for industrialized purposes, this is one of the last remnants of the coastal wetlands and marshes that once stretched along the entire shoreline.

The Green Necklace is another unique urban greenway. Its origins go back almost to the beginning of the District. One of the principal landowners in the early days was Edward Mahon, whose North Vancouver Land and Improvement Company (NVLIC) held many properties in the lower Lonsdale area. Mahon was inspired by the City Beautiful movement in the United States

This plan, from a 1908 pamphlet, shows an idealized version of Grand Boulevard. The view looks south across Burrard Inlet, emphasizing the spaciousness and elegance of what was supposed to be North Vancouver's most affluent residential neighbourhood. NVMA Pamphlet 1908-2

The Lynn Valley streetcar trundles up the middle of Grand Boulevard in June, 1946. Three months later voters in a plebiscite approved the replacement of the streetcar system with motor buses. NVMA 6559

and the garden city movement in the United Kingdom. Both of these planning movements hoped to make communities more liveable by incorporating green spaces, gardens and parks into urban settings, and Mahon wanted to bring some of their ideas to the North Shore. He planned a network of parks and boulevards that would encircle the community and, in his words, act like "a great artificial lung . . . breathing, pressing, forcing into it health and vitality."[38] The project kicked off in 1905 when volunteers began clearing land at Keith Road and Lonsdale that was donated by the NVLIC and another developer, Alfred St. George Hamersley. This eventually became Victoria Park, a picturesque promenade right in the middle of the city. Mahon's group next began to develop a subdivision on West 6th Street that was envisioned as an upscale residential district for affluent families. Known as "Ottawa Gardens," it featured a wide boulevard that linked to the green necklace plan.

But the jewel in the "necklace" was the

The playground at Cates Park/Whey-ah-Wichen, the largest waterfront park in the District, jointly managed with the Tsleil-Waututh First Nation.
Courtesy of the District of North Vancouver

Grand Boulevard, a broad, manicured parkway intended quite consciously to rival the Champs-Élysées in Paris or Unter den Linden in Berlin. Designed in 1906 as another upscale residential neighbourhood, the boulevard offers panoramic views of the inlet and Vancouver beyond. At 105.5 metres in width, it remains the widest landscaped city street in the province. It also provided a firebreak between Lynn Valley, where logging and sawmilling were active industries, and the City of North Vancouver. In 1907 the street railway ran track up the middle of the boulevard so that residents could be within minutes of the ferry dock. When the line was later removed, it was replaced by a footpath that now meanders down the boulevard. Despite the work that went into beautifying the boulevard, it failed to attract the sort of well-to-do homebuyer originally intended. There were simply not that many people wealthy enough, especially when the recession hit in 1913, and much of the land on either side of the park remained forested well into the 1920s, when residential

Above: The Capilano Bridge on the Upper Levels Highway under construction. For several kilometres east from the Capilano River the new highway cut right through the heart of the District. VPL 45455

Right: Premier W. A. C. Bennett (c.) cuts the ribbon at the official opening of the Upper Levels Highway on March 4, 1961. VPL 45432 construction picked up again. Today, with its landscaped central corridor and many stately homes, Grand Boulevard fulfills the aspirations of its original developers.

Meanwhile, the northern section of the Green Necklace was left uncompleted. The construction of the Upper Levels Highway from 1959 to 1960 brought one major interruption to the plan. The highway, which stretches the length of the North Shore from Horseshoe Bay to the Second Narrows Bridge, had a paradoxical effect. On the one hand, when it opened on March 4, 1961, it made it possible to drive from one side of the District to the other in a matter of minutes, linking neighbourhoods and contributing to the emergence of a unified North Vancouver identity. On the other hand, the roadway drove right through the middle of the community. In West Vancouver the impact was less extreme since the highway was laid out to the north of most of the residential areas. In North Vancouver, however, engineers chose the most direct route between the Capilano River and the Second Narrows, which meant that the highway divided residential areas such as Pemberton Heights and Capilano Heights. Many properties were expropriated to make way for construction, and in the eastern side of the District the route, now known to commuters as "The Cut," overwhelmed Keith Creek, a popular nature area that otherwise would naturally have formed part of the Green Necklace.

The track and playing fields at Sutherland Secondary are well-used outdoor recreational facilities for North Vancouver youngsters.
Alexandra Greenberg photo

North Vancouver has always been a place for hikers to get out into the wilderness within easy reach of the city. Here members of the BC Mountaineering Club pose at the top of Crown Mountain in January 1929.
NVMA 13011

More recently, civic officials have announced plans to finish construction of the Necklace. When it is done, there will be a green loop stretching 7 kilometres around the central core of the City, fulfilling a 100-year-old promise to the citizens of the North Shore. One important link in the Green Necklace is Mahon Park, named for Edward Mahon and sold to the city by his North Vancouver Land and Improvement Company in 1910. The park grew to include a track and dance pavilion and remains one of the city's major recreational facilities.

There are many hiking trails on the North Shore, but two merit special mention. One is the Baden-Powell Trail, a rugged path that winds its way for 48 kilometres across the face of the North Shore Mountains, from Deep Cove in the east to Horseshoe Bay in the west. Named for Lord Baden-Powell, the founder of the scouting movement, the trail was initiated by BC's Boy Scouts and Girl Guides in 1971 to celebrate the centennial of the province's entry into Canadian Confederation. Much of the work was done by the youngsters but they had a lot of help from other community groups and individuals.

Down closer to the waterfront is the North Shore Spirit Trail. When completed, it will also run from Horseshoe Bay to Deep Cove, but unlike the Baden-Powell Trail, the Spirit Trail runs right through the heart of the community. It is a 35-km-long water-oriented pathway accommodating walkers, joggers, cyclists, and inline skaters as well as people with mobility aids. In a sense, the trail reunites the original District of North Vancouver, which once included the entire waterfront from Howe Sound to Indian Arm.

The Spirit Trail is part of a wider initiative: the reclamation of parts of the North Shore waterfront for recreational use. North Vancouver began as a mill town, and from its earliest days, the waterfront has been occupied by a variety of port-related industries: sawmills, grain silos, rail lines, shipyards, chemical plants and cargo terminals. Much of the original shoreline was filled in over the years to accommodate these activities, which have been the economic lifeblood of the North Shore. More recently, however, the community has expressed a desire to balance its industrial needs with enhanced waterfront recreational opportunities. Projects such as the Spirit Trail, Whey-ah-Wichen, the heritage shipyard district, the Maplewood Conservation Area, and the

Waterfront Park (which was once occupied by a sawmill) all reflect this new waterfront orientation. At the same time, successful attempts have been made to reclaim some of the streams that have been befouled with industrial waste and degraded by urban development. Today, thanks to the work of many volunteers, salmon are once again spawning in places that only a generation ago could not support any fish at all. All of these projects reflect a renewed commitment to North Vancouver's identity as a place where people live "at nature's edge."

"There has to be park facilities or squares where the public can express themselves. A source and opportunity for expression. There has to be a place for a centre. We definitely have to have places where we can gather as a public, as a society, where we can gather around and express our views."
—Dirk Oostindie, District parks superintendent 1959–1993[39]

Since the 1980s, snowboarding has joined skiing as a popular winter sport on the North Shore mountains. Kevin Sansalone photo

TOP OF GROUSE MTN.
1906

Conclusion

Communities such as North Vancouver have been called "wilderburbs,"[40] places where suburban development borders abruptly on wilderness areas. Located at the interface between urban, suburban and not urban at all, "wilderburbs" combine the density, and intensity, of city living with the wide open spaces of the back of beyond. There are not many communities like North Vancouver where nature intrudes so insistently into daily life, where going "back to nature" is as easy as walking out the back door and seeing black bears amble nonchalantly through the garden gate. For many residents, wilderburbs combine the best of two worlds: the creature comforts of urban living with the rougher attractions of wild nature.

North Vancouver is unique for its location. Spread across the south-facing mountain slopes overlooking one of the busiest harbours in the world, the community is within an easy commute of the urban centre of Vancouver, regularly chosen as one of the world's most liveable cities. Yet most North Vancouverites identify the natural environment—the mountains, the forests, the creeks and the wilderness areas—as the defining elements of their community, the reason why they appreciate living here. The iconic images of the North Shore—the twin peaks of the Lions, the brightly lit ski slopes of Grouse Mountain—speak to the community's pride in its closeness to the outdoors and outdoor activity. From the beginning, the North Shore was valued for its wilderness resources: the fresh, clean water that gushes from taps all over the Lower Mainland and the tall timber that produced the wood that built so many homes. North Vancouver has also contributed to the collection of images that residents of the Lower Mainland use to describe themselves. Famously we are the place where two worlds coexist, where people ski in the morning and sail in the afternoon, where the hinterland is never more than a few minutes away.

Yet these images of a wilderness playground cannot obscure the destructive side of the community's history. It is a paradox that while North Vancouver has been valued as a place to commune with nature, it has also been a place where the natural environment has been exploited and destroyed. The Squamish and the Tsleil-Waututh lived for generations at their camps and settlements along the shores of Burrard Inlet without degrading the complex ecology of the region. With the arrival of outsiders, however, the balance shifted. Forests were denuded to provide wood products for local building and for export, leading to excess runoff, flooding and water contamination. Creeks became uninhabitable for their stocks of salmon and trout. Meanwhile, on the waterfront, industrial activity connected to the port completely transformed the shoreline. Many kilometres of pristine wetlands were filled in and dredged up to make way for mills, cargo terminals, railway tracks, grain

Opposite: The North Vancouver mountains have always been a destination for urbanites in search of wilderness recreation. This group of hikers poses near the top of Grouse Mountain in 1906. NVMA 55

The North Vancouver waterfront is part of the Port of Vancouver, the busiest harbour in Canada. Lisa Wilson photo

silos and chemical plants. The shoreline that exists today in no way resembles the natural shoreline once used by the First Nations to harvest shellfish and hunt waterfowl.

The history of North Vancouver during its first 125 years resembles the swing of a pendulum. Relations with the First Nations people are a case in point. Once settlement began in earnest, the dominant majority forced the original inhabitants to the margins. The needs of the First Nations were ignored. Their lands were expropriated, their culture demeaned. The people were forced onto reserves and into the residential schools in an attempt to acculturate them to the mainstream. But in the past few decades the pendulum has swung in the other direction. Today there is a growing realization in the non-Aboriginal community that it is time to reconcile with the First Nations and work with them as partners, not in order to forget the past but in order to begin the long process of developing a more respectful relationship.

Similarly, the attitude to the natural environment has gone through a profound change. When the District was created in 1891, its land base was viewed as a vast cornucopia overflowing with a wealth of natural resources: timber, minerals, seafood and wildlife. Very little restraint was shown in plundering these resources and landscapes in the name of economic development. More recently, residents of the North Shore have recognized that they are custodians of a unique natural environment and have committed to protecting it by taking a more sustainable approach to economic development. There is no going back. The port-related industries that so transformed the waterfront are the economic lifeblood of the community; they are here to stay. But successful efforts to reinvigorate some of the shoreline, preserve significant amounts of parkland and reclaim the rivers and creeks all speak to a future for North Vancouver that seeks to be very different from its past.

Endnotes

1 Major James Skitt Matthews, *Early Vancouver*, vol. 2 (Vancouver: City of Vancouver, 2011), 22.
2 Tomas Bartroli, *Genesis of Vancouver City* (Vancouver: self-published, 1987), 70.
3 Ibid., 100.
4 Jean Barman, *Stanley Park's Secret* (Madeira Park, BC: Harbour Publishing, 2005), 40.
5 *Man Along the Shore!* (Vancouver: ILWU Local 500 Pensioners, 1975), 13.
6 C. J. Taylor, "Moodyville and Hastings Mill," Historic Sites and Monuments Board Agenda Paper, 1988, p.93.
7 Simon Baker, *Khot-La-Cha: The Autobiography of Chief Simon Baker* (Vancouver: Douglas & McIntyre, 1994), 2.
8 Thomas Diplock, "The North Shore As I Knew It from 1897," Unpublished memoir, North Vancouver Museum & Archives, Item 560.
9 James Delgado, *Waterfront* (Vancouver: Stanton, Atkins & Dosil, 2005), 40.
10 *Man Along the Shore!* op. cit., 66.
11 *North Shore Express*, April 14, 1911, p.4.
12 Kathleen Woodward-Reynolds, *A History of the City and District of North Vancouver* (Vancouver: UBC, MA thesis, 1943), 81.
13 Walter Draycott, *Early Days in Lynn Valley* (North Vancouver: District of North Vancouver, 2000), 26.
14 *North Vancouver News*, August 19, 1955, p.12.
15 Dennis Reid, *A Concise History of Canadian Painting* (Toronto: Oxford University Press, 1988), 196.
16 Sean Kheraj, *Inventing Stanley Park* (Vancouver: UBC Press, 2013), 139.
17 James W. Morton, *Capilano: The Story of a River* (Toronto: McClelland & Stewart, 1970), 77.
18 Draycott, op. cit., 30.
19 Woodward-Reynolds, op. cit., 78.
20 Dawn Sparks and Martha Border, *Echoes Across the Inlet* (District of North Vancouver: Deep Cove and Area Heritage Association, 1989), 22.
21 Ibid., 74.
22 Interview transcript, North Vancouver Museum & Archives.
23 Ibid.
24 Donald Luxton, *The Modern Architecture of North Vancouver, 1930–1965* (North Vancouver: District of North Vancouver, 1997), 6.
25 Interview transcript, North Vancouver Museum & Archives.
26 Ibid.
27 Ibid.
28 Ibid.
29 Karl Newholm, "North Vancouver City and District: The Amalgamation Issue," unpublished paper, North Vancouver Museum & Archives, Item 672, 1987, p.2.
30 Warren Sommer, *The Ambitious City* (Madeira Park, BC: Harbour Publishing, 2007), 302.
31 Baker, op. cit., 98.
32 Lilia D'Acres and Donald Luxton, *Lions Gate* (Vancouver: Talonbooks, 1999), 141.
33 Baker, op. cit., 10.
34 Interview transcript, North Vancouver Museum & Archives.
35 *Vancouver Sun*, July 2, 2015.
36 Kathryn Bridge, *Phyllis Munday: Mountaineer* (Lantzville, BC: XYZ Publishing, 2002), 43.
37 Morton, op. cit., 58.
38 Walter Volovsek, *The Green Necklace* (Castlegar, BC: Otmar Publishing, 2012), 116.
39 Interview transcript, North Vancouver Museum & Archives.
40 The term "wilderburb" is borrowed from Lincoln Bramwell, *Wilderburbs: Communities on Nature's Edge* (Seattle: University of Washington Press, 2014).

About This Book

This book is a project of the North Vancouver Museum & Archives (NVMA). As a municipal heritage organization that explores history, connects people and shares ideas, NVMA encourages community members to contribute to the historical record.

Our "Voices and Views" outreach project invited current and former residents to share their personal stories, family histories and photographs of North Vancouver. In an online exhibit (found at http://www.nvma.ca) and the pages of *Where Mountains Meet the Sea*, these contributions—together with photographs of Museum artifacts—help bring to life a past that is connected to individual experiences. Because 2016 is the quasquicentennial of North Vancouver District, *Where Mountains Meet the Sea* naturally focuses on the history of that community. (There is already an excellent history of the City, *The Ambitious City: A History of the City of North Vancouver*, by Warren Sommer.) That said, the present volume includes the story of the City, and to a lesser extent of West Vancouver, where it seems appropriate to do so. Their histories are so intertwined as to be almost impossible to separate.

A non-traditional, non-chronological history book, *Where Mountains Meet the Sea* has been researched and beautifully written by historian Daniel Francis. Dan's enthusiasm for the rich and layered history of North Vancouver District, where he lives, is evident throughout the book's pages. We thank him for making this project so rewarding for all involved.

Generous financial support for *Where Mountains Meet the Sea* and the 125th anniversary community engagement project was received from the British Columbia Arts Council, the District of North Vancouver, the Kitty Heller Estate, the Canada Summer Jobs program and the Friends of the North Vancouver Museum & Archives Society.

—Nancy Kirkpatrick
Director, North Vancouver Museum & Archives

NORTH VANCOUVER DISTRICT

FRIENDS SOCIETY nvma NORTH VANCOUVER MUSEUM & ARCHIVES

Sources

The North Vancouver Museum & Archives (NVMA) contains a wealth of primary source material about all aspects of North Vancouver history, too numerous to be listed below. The author wishes to thank archivist Janet Turner, reference historian Daien Ide, curator Karen Dearlove, community engagement curator Lisa Wilson, museum director Nancy Kirkpatrick and museum assistant director Shirley Sutherland for all their advice and assistance. Nancy, Janet and Shirley read an early draft of the book and made many useful suggestions for improvements, as did District Mayor Richard Walton, a long-time resident of the North Shore. Thanks also to Sanford Osler, Sheryl Fisher and Robert Watt, who also read an early draft, and to Anna Gooding, who assisted with image collection.

A great deal of the information in *Where Mountains Meet the Sea* was gathered from interviews with residents of the District and City carried out over a number of years by a variety of interviewers. These interviews, some of them transcribed, can be accessed at the NVMA.

The author was helped greatly by research done over the years by local historian Roy Pallant. A particularly useful source was the *Visions of North Shore*, a research project carried out in 1999–2000 exploring the history of twelve neighbourhoods across the North Shore. The project resulted in a series of annotated essays, edited by Laura Millar, and available at the NVMA.

General written sources include Doreen Armitage, *Burrard Inlet: A History* (Madeira Park, BC: Harbour Publishing, 2001); Robert E. Cail, *Land, Man and the Law: The Disposal of Crown Lands in British Columbia , 1871–1913* (Vancouver: UBC Press, 1974); Chuck Davis, *Reflections—One Hundred Years: A Celebration of the District of North Vancouver's Centennial* (Vancouver: Opus Productions, 1990); Sharon Proctor, *Time Travel in North Vancouver* (Surrey, BC: Hancock House, 2010); Shervin Shahriari, *North Vancouver's Lonsdale Neighbourhood* (Charleston, SC: Arcadia Publishing, 2009); Warren Sommer, *The Ambitious City: A History of the City of North Vancouver* (Madeira Park, BC: Harbour Publishing, 2007); and Marjorie Woodward-Reynolds, *A History of the City and District of North Vancouver* (MA thesis, UBC, 1943). A number of relevant planning documents are available on the websites of the City and the District. More specific studies are listed below under the relevant chapters.

Chapter One

Useful accounts of the visits to Burrard Inlet by the early European explorers are Tomas Bartroli, *Genesis of Vancouver City: Explorations of Its Site 1791, 1792 & 1808* (Vancouver: self-published, 1997); Robin Fisher, *Vancouver's Voyage: Charting the Northwest Coast, 1791–1795* (Vancouver: Douglas & McIntyre, 1992); and Jim McDowell, *Uncharted Waters: the Explorations of José Narváez, 1768–1840* (Vancouver: Ronsdale Press, 2015). Accounts of the First Nations occupation are in Jean Barman, *Stanley Park's Secret: The Forgotten Families of Whoi Whoi, Kanaka Ranch and Brockton Point* (Madeira Park, BC: Harbour Publishing, 2005) and Jesse Morin, "Tsleil-Waututh Nation's History, Culture and Aboriginal Interests in Eastern Burrard Inlet" (May 2015, available online through the Sacred Trust). Also useful is Pauline Johnson, *Legends of Vancouver* (Vancouver: Douglas & McIntyre, 1997, originally published 1911) and Major James Skitt Matthews, *Early Vancouver*, vol 2. (Vancouver: City of Vancouver, 2011). Sources on the history of Moodyville are A. L. Lazenby, *Moody and Moodyville* (unpublished manuscript, North Vancouver Museum & Archives Library, 2010); C. James Taylor, "Moodyville and Hastings Mill: Historic Burrard Inlet Sawmill" (unpublished Agenda Paper, Historic Sites and Monuments Board of Canada, Ottawa 1988); F. W. Howay, "Early Settlements on Burrard Inlet," *BC Historical Quarterly* (April 1937), 101–14; and James W. Morton, *The Enterprising Mr. Moody, the Bumptious Captain Stamp* (Vancouver: J. J. Douglas, 1977). In *Waterfront: The Illustrated Maritime Story of Greater Vancouver* (Vancouver: Stanton, Atkins & Dosil, 2005), James P. Delgado offers an illustrated history of developments around the harbour, including on the North Shore. First-hand accounts of longshoring are in Ben Swankey, *"Man Along the Shore!": the Story of the Vancouver Waterfront* (Vancouver: ILWU Local 500, 1975). For early settlement in West Vancouver, see Francis Mansbridge, *Cottages to Communities: The Story of West Vancouver's Neighbourhoods* (West Vancouver: West Vancouver Historical Society, 2011) and Elspeth Bradbury, *West Vancouver: A View Through the Trees* (West Vancouver: District of West Vancouver, 2007). The different ferries are described in Capt. James Barr, *Ferry Across the Harbor: The Story of the North Vancouver Ferries* (Vancouver: Mitchell Press, 1969) and John R. Burnes, *Echoes of the Ferries: A History of the North Vancouver Ferry Service* (n.p., n.d.). For the North Shore bridges, see Eric Jamieson, *Tragedy at Second Narrows: The Story of the Ironworkers Memorial Bridge* (Madeira Park, BC: Harbour Publishing, 2008) and Lilia D'Acres and Donald Luxton, *Lions Gate* (Burnaby: Talonbooks, 1999). Shipbuilding is the subject of Francis Mansbridge, *Launching History: The Saga of Burrard Dry Dock* (Madeira Park, BC: Harbour Publishing, 2002) and T. A. McLaren and Vickie Jensen, *Ships of Steel: A British Columbia Shipbuilder's Story* (Madeira Park, BC: Harbour Publishing, 2000). Also useful was F. G. Architectural and Planning Consultants, *Versatile Pacific Shipyards Heritage Report* (1991). The story of the PGE Railway on the North Shore is told in Patrick O. Hind, *The Pacific Great Eastern Railway: A Short History of the North Shore Subdivision, 1914–1928* (North Vancouver: North Vancouver Museum & Archives Commission, 1999), while developments in the port are in John Everitt and Warren Gill, "The Early Development of Terminal Grain Elevators on Canada's Pacific Coast," *Western Geography* 15/16 (2005/2006), 28–52, and Transport Canada, *Planning Lasting Infrastructure* (SNC Lavalin: North Shore Trade Area Study Final Report, September 30, 2008).

Chapter Two

Political developments in early North Vancouver are described in John R. Burnes, *North Vancouver, 1891–1907: Saga of a Municipality in its Formative Days* (North Vancouver: n.p., 1970). The streetcars are the subject of Henry Ewert, *The Perfect Little Streetcar System* (North Vancouver: North Vancouver Museum Commission, 2000). Descriptions of the different neighbourhoods are in Donald J. Bourdon, *The Boom Years: G. G. Nye's Photographs of North Vancouver 1905–1909* (North Vancouver: Hancock House, 1981); Thomas B. Diplock, "The North Shore As I Knew It from 1897" (unpublished typescript, North Vancouver Museum & Archives, Item 560, 1978); Walter Draycott, *Early Days in Lynn Valley* (North Vancouver: District of North Vancouver, 2000, 2nd ed.); Fred Hollingsworth, *Living Spaces: the Architecture of Fred Thornton Hollingsworth* (Vancouver: Blueimprint, 2005); Donald Luxton, *The Modern Architecture of North Vancouver, 1930–1965* (North Vancouver: District of North Vancouver, 1998); James W. Morton, *Capilano:*

The Story of a River (Toronto: McClelland and Stewart, 1970); Janet Pavlik, *Echoes Across Seymour: A History of North Vancouver's Eastern Communities Including Dollarton and Deep Cove* (Madeira Park, BC: Harbour Publishing, 2012); and Dawn Sparks and Martha Border, *Echoes Across the Inlet* (North Vancouver: Deep Cove and Area Heritage Association, 1989). Early logging in the Capilano, Lynn Creek and Seymour watersheds is detailed in Thomas B. Diplock, "Some Recollections of Early Days in the Sawmill Business on the North Shore" (unpublished paper, North Vancouver Museum & Archives, Item 560, n.d.); in three studies by Gabrielle Kahrer: "A Historical Geography of Logging Along Lynn Creek: 1870s to 1928" (unpublished paper, April 1987, North Vancouver Museum & Archives); "Logging and Landscape Change on the North Shore of Burrard Inlet, 1860s–1930s" (MA thesis, University of British Columbia, Dept. of Geography, 1988); *From Speculative to Spectacular: The Seymour River Valley 1870s to 1980s. A History of Resource Use* (Burnaby: Greater Vancouver Regional District Parks Department, 1989); and David M. Rees-Thomas, *Timber Down the Capilano: A History of the Capilano Timber Company* (Victoria: British Columbia Railway Historical Society, 1979). Gray Scrimgeour tells the story of maritime postal delivery in "Burrard Inlet (2) Revisited," *Postal History Society of Canada Journal,* No. 141 (Spring 2010), 3–14. The most complete history of Indian Arm is Ralph Drew, *Ferries & Fjord: The History of Indian Arm, Its Ferries & Docks, Travelling Post Offices & Floating Grocery Stores* (Belcarra: s.p., 2015). Along with James W. Morton, the opening of the Capilano reservoir is in Louis P. Cain, "Water and Sanitation Services in Vancouver: An Historical Perspective," *BC Studies* 30 (Summer 1976), 27–43, and Sean Kheraj, *Inventing Stanley Park: An Environmental History* (Vancouver: UBC Press, 2013). The story of the Blair Rifle Range is described in detail in Donna Sacuta, "Building Andy's Range: The History of the Blair Rifle Range in North Vancouver" (2014, available online through the Deep Cove Heritage Society). Wartime housing is the subject of two studies by Jill Wade: "Wartime Housing Limited, 1941–47: Canadian Housing Policy at the Crossroads" (MA thesis, Dept. of History, University of British Columbia, 1984) and *Houses for All: The Struggle for Social Housing in Vancouver, 1919–1950* (Vancouver: UBC Press, 1994). Wartime defences on the North Shore are detailed in Peter N. Moogk, *Vancouver Defended: A History of Men and Guns of the Lower Mainland Defences, 1859–1945* (Vancouver: Antonson Publishing Ltd., 1978). The history of Cates Park (Whey-ah-Wichen), as First Nations home, industrial site and parkland, is in Tsleil-Waututh Nation and District of North Vancouver, *Cates Park/Whey-ah-Wichen Park Master Plan and Cultural Resources Interpretation Master Plan* (North Vancouver: May 2006). Sally Carswell describes the development of a public hospital on the North Shore in her *The Story of Lions Gate Hospital* (West Vancouver: Carswell and Carswell, 1980). The history of the library system is the subject of Don Obee's *Fifty! With a Fabulous Future: A History of the North Vancouver District Public Library* (North Vancouver: NVDPL, 2014). The story of the squatters' shacks is in Sheryl Salloum, *Malcolm Lowry, Vancouver Days* (Madeira Park, BC: Harbour Publishing, 1987) and by the same author, "The By-Gone Days of Dollarton," *Raincoast Chronicles 15* (Madeira Park, BC: Harbour Publishing, 1993: 68–77), as well as *West of Eden* (North Vancouver: Presentation House Gallery, 2014). The politics of re-amalgamation are discussed in Karl Newholm, "North Vancouver City and District: The Amalgamation Issue" (unpublished paper, 31 March 1987, North Vancouver Museum & Archives, Item 672). The First Nations communities are the subject of Simon Baker, *Khot-La-Cha: The Autobiography of Chief Simon Baker* (Vancouver: Douglas & McIntyre, 1994) and Thomas Lascelles, *Mission on the Inlet:*

St. Paul's Indian Catholic Church, North Vancouver, BC, 1863–1984 (Vancouver: Oblates of Mary Immaculate, 1984). *From Far and Wide: Cultural Diversity in North Vancouver* (City of North Vancouver, 2015) by Warren Sommer, describes the different cultural communities in North Vancouver.

Chapter Three

For coastal mountaineering, see Susan Leslie, ed., *In the Western Mountains: Early Mountaineering in British Columbia* (Sound Heritage Series, vol. VIII, No. 4, 1980) and Francis Mansbridge, *Hollyburn: The Mountain and the City* (Vancouver: Ronsdale Press, 2008). As well, the Mount Seymour History Project (www.mtseymourhistory.ca) contains a wealth of information about cabin culture on the mountains. Along with Morton's *Capilano*, a valuable source of information about recreation and tourism in the Capilano Valley is Donald J. Bourdon, "Early Recreational Businesses in Capilano, North Vancouver, BC, 1900–1939" (unpublished paper, 1975, North Vancouver Museum & Archives 684). See also Eleanore Dempster, *The Laughing Bridge: A Personal History of the Capilano Suspension Bridge* (Maple Ridge: Impressions in Print, 1988) for an account of the suspension bridge. The pre-history of North Shore Rescue is in Paddy Sherman, "Formation of the Mountain Rescue Group," *Canadian Alpine Journal*, vol. XL (1957), 87–89. The origins of the Green Necklace, indeed the origins of North Vancouver, are described in Walter O. Volovsek, *The Green Necklace: The Vision Quest of Edward Mahon* (Castlegar: Otmar Publishing, 2012).

Chauffeur Harry Stevens and guests in the 1912 Mitchell touring car that taxied visitors to and from the Canyon View Hotel, located at the site of today's Cleveland Dam, ca. 1914. NVMA 6724

Index

1 2 3 4 5 — 20 19 18 17 16

Harbour Publishing Co. Ltd.
P.O. Box 219, Madeira Park, BC, V0N 2H0
www.harbourpublishing.com

Endsheets: Courtesy of North Vancouver Museum and Archives, NVMA 1926-10
Edited by Nicola Goshulak
Indexed by Brianna Cerkiewicz
Text design by Roger Handling
Dust jacket design by Shed Simas
Printed and bound in Canada
Printed on paper certified by the Forest Stewardship Council

Canada Council for the Arts | Conseil des Arts du Canada | British Columbia Arts Council — An agency of the Province of British Columbia | Canada

Harbour Publishing acknowledges the support of the Canada Council for the Arts, which last year invested $153 million to bring the arts to Canadians throughout the country. We also gratefully acknowledge financial support from the Government of Canada through the Canada Book Fund and from the Province of British Columbia through the BC Arts Council and the Book Publishing Tax Credit.

Cataloguing data available from Library and Archives Canada
ISBN 978-1-55017-751-0 (cloth)
ISBN 978-1-55017-752-7 (ebook)

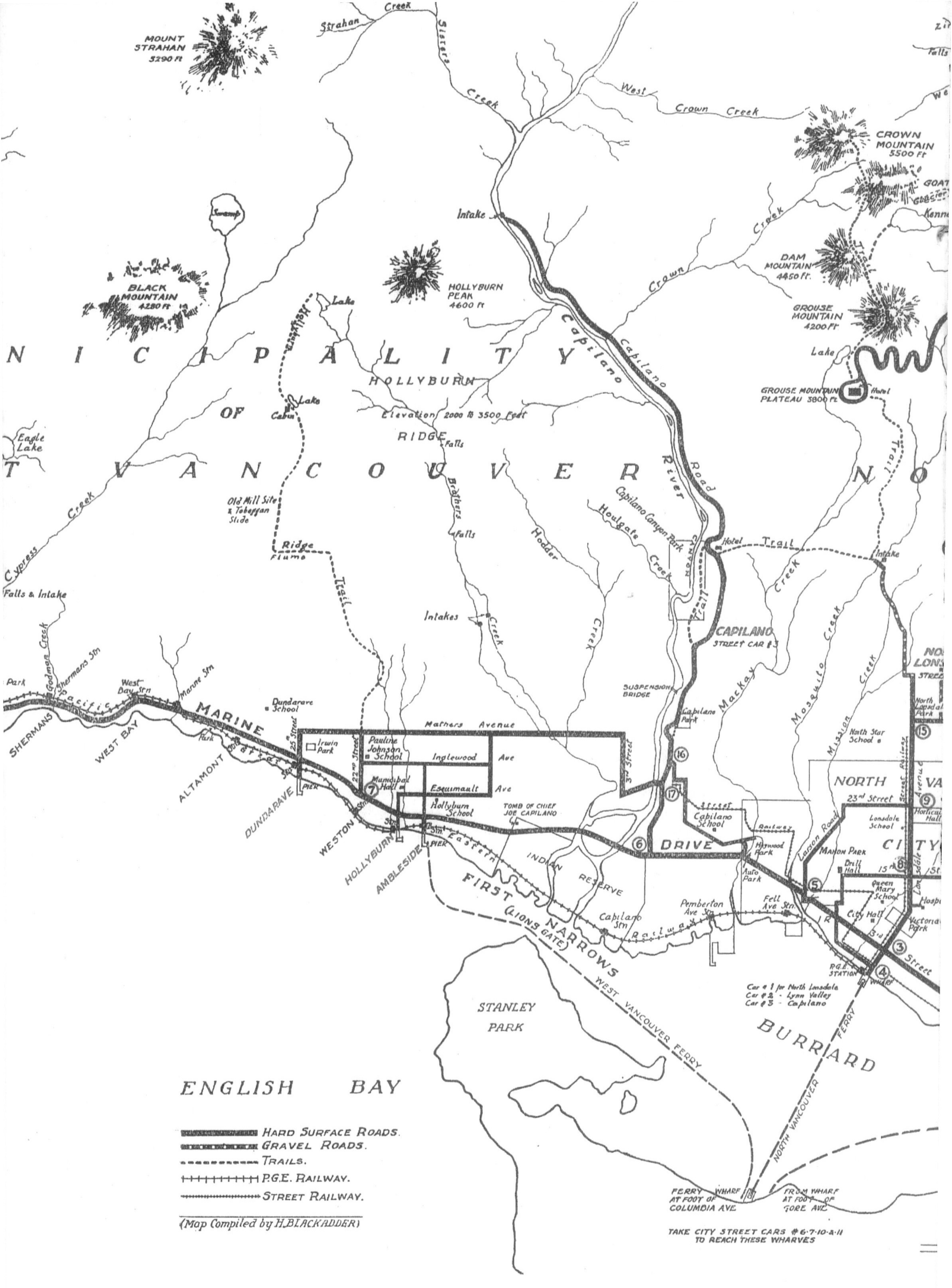
MOUNT STRAHAN 5290 Ft
Strahan Creek
Sisters Creek
West Crown Creek
CROWN MOUNTAIN 5500 Ft
Intake
HOLLYBURN PEAK 4600 Ft
BLACK MOUNTAIN 4280 Ft
Swamp
DAM MOUNTAIN 4450 Ft.
GROUSE MOUNTAIN 4200 Ft
Crown Creek
Capilano
Capilano River
Capilano Road
Lake
GROUSE MOUNTAIN PLATEAU 3800 Ft
Hotel
Trail
NICIPALITY OF
T VANCOUVER
NO
HOLLYBURN
Elevation 2000 to 3500 Feet
RIDGE
Falls
Lake
Cabin
Eagle Lake
Cypress Creek
Falls & Intake
Old Mill Site & Toboggan Slide
Ridge Flume
Trail
Brothers
Falls
Hodder
Capilano Canyon Park
Houlgate Creek
Hotel
Trail
Intake
Intakes
Creek
CAPILANO
STREET CAR # 3
Mackay
Mosquito Creek
Mission Creek
SUSPENSION BRIDGE
Capilano Park
Park
Godman Creek
Shermans Stn
West Bay Stn
Marine Stn
Pacific
Dundarave School
MARINE
SHERMANS
WEST BAY
ALTAMONT
DUNDARAVE
PIER
25th Street
Irwin Park
22nd Street
Pauline Johnson School
Municipal Hall
Mathers Avenue
Inglewood Ave
Esquimault Ave
Hollyburn School
TOMB OF CHIEF JOE CAPILANO
3rd Street
WESTON
HOLLYBURN
AMBLESIDE
Eastern
INDIAN RESERVE
DRIVE
Capilano School
Street Railway
Heywood Park
Auto Park
FIRST NARROWS (LIONS GATE)
Capilano Stn
Pemberton Ave Stn
Fell Ave Stn
Railway
North Star School
NORTH VA
23rd Street
Lonsdale School
Larson Road
MAHON PARK
Drill Hall
CITY
15th St
Queen Mary School
City Hall
Victoria Park
P.G.E. STATION
Wharf
Street
Car # 1 for North Lonsdale
Car # 2 - Lynn Valley
Car # 3 - Capilano
STANLEY PARK
WEST VANCOUVER FERRY
BURRARD
NORTH VANCOUVER FERRY
ENGLISH BAY
HARD SURFACE ROADS.
GRAVEL ROADS.
TRAILS.
P.G.E. RAILWAY.
STREET RAILWAY.
(Map Compiled by H. BLACKADDER)
FERRY WHARF AT FOOT OF COLUMBIA AVE.
FROM WHARF AT FOOT OF GORE AVE.
TAKE CITY STREET CARS # 6·7·10·&·11 TO REACH THESE WHARVES